Mr. Tony's Lessons of *La Famiglia*

Lynn Byrd

with contributing writer
Phillip Marshall

Copyright © 2005 James W. Rane

All rights reserved. No part of this book may be reproduced or transmitted in any form or by any means, electronic or mechanical, including photocopying, recording or by any information storage or retrieval system, without permission from the publisher.

*Published by Cottagegate Books
(a division of Perkins Creative, Inc.)
177 Rabbit Farm Trail
Advance, NC 27006*

All trademarks and service marks appearing herein are the property of their respective owners and their appearance herein does not imply that the goods or services identified by such marks originate from, are affiliated with, or are endorsed by the author, publisher, copyright holder, or sponsor of this publication or that this publication originates from, is affiliated with, or is sponsored by the owners of said marks.

The photographs and images contained in this book are either the property of the Rane family, used herein with permission (Corbis/Bettman Archives, Mike Rivers and the Wisconsin Historical Society), or otherwise in the public domain.

*Contributing Writer: Phillip Marshall.
Additional images provided by Rick Douglas and Ricky Perkins.
Art Direction, Layout and Design: Rick Douglas.
Italian translations: Tony Econ.*

ISBN 0-9773887-0-0

Printed in the United States of America.

10 9 8 7 6 5 4 3 2 1

This book was set in Union.

FOREWORD

As we go through life we will meet many people. Many will pass on through our lives and be gone forever. Still others will become a pleasant memory. Once in a great while you will shake hands with a man and realize you just shook hands with a friend. I later read a book about such a friend and discovered, not only was I right, but also he is a great American, a faithful husband and loving father. Tony Rane is a man I am proud to call my friend.

Dale Robertson,
Star of *Tales of Wells Fargo*

"Una buona vita
dura pi lungamente
di un corso della vita."

– A good life lasts longer than a lifetime.

Contents

Introduction	The Kitchen	1
Chapter 1	A Sweet Life	2
Chapter 2	A Humble Beginning	5
Chapter 3	Giuseppe Becomes Joseph	8
Chapter 4	The 'Bush	14
Chapter 5	Figs and Bees	22
Chapter 6	The Name of the Boat	26
Chapter 7	The Biggest and Best Surprise	37
Chapter 8	Ghosts	43
Chapter 9	Wine 101	48
Chapter 10	The Watermelon Heist	54
Chapter 11	Quitting Is Not An Option	60
Chapter 12	Be An American	64
Chapter 13	Itchy Feet	74
Chapter 14	Big City Lessons	78
Chapter 15	The Call to Duty	90
Chapter 16	Love and War	98
Chapter 17	The Value of a Perfect Song	112
Chapter 18	Good Food, Good Town, Good Times	118
Chapter 19	Remember The Elysee	132
Chapter 20	A Family Affair	158
Chapter 21	Great Southern Lives Up to Its Name	172
Chapter 22	The Hard Tenderhearted Lessons	186
Chapter 23	God Is In Every House	202
Chapter 24	La Famiglia	208
Chapter 25	The Eternal Optimist	216
Epilogue	The Saucepot	224
Acknowledgments		226

The kitchen

in Jimmy and Angela Rane's house is filled with people. Excellent appetizers in the family room are, for the most part, ignored, and so are the comfortable chairs. Everyone is gathered around the kitchen bar, standing, waiting. We all take turns casually sneaking by the stove and lifting the lid from a pot of Mr. Tony's spaghetti sauce. This simple action causes everyone to subconsciously inhale the aroma of, well, love. Mr. Tony's sauce is spellbinding. There is no world outside of that warm and cozy kitchen that requires immediate attention; all thoughts are turned to comfort food. Simple fare, this spaghetti. But simple is never to be confused with easy. Simple is divine. This recipe of Mr. Tony's goes far beyond opening a jar of Ragu.

"This is my mother's recipe," says Mr. Tony. "She brought it from Italy, and I grew up on it. Now, Jimmy and Greg have learned how to make it. We do it together in a big batch, and it takes all day. The secret is, well, I can't tell you that."

So we are content to eat and to hope that someday the recipe might slip into our hands, and our own families will be filled with Mr. Tony's love, too; we hope that maybe someday we will become romantic Italians through osmosis.

CHAPTER I

Abbeville, Alabama, USA, July 2004

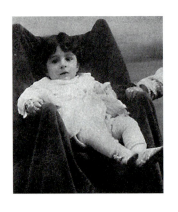

**Anthony Rane,
in Greenbush, 1917.**

Eighty-eight-year-old Anthony J. Rane, known as Mr. Tony to his family and many friends, has never met a stranger. Although macular degeneration has robbed Mr. Tony of clear vision, he greets his visitors at the door, offers a gently firm handshake, and looks them dead in the eye.

"I cannot read my own mail," Mr. Tony says. "My wife and children open everything and read it to me. So, no. I can't read email, but I hate computers anyway. We'll have to communicate the old-fashioned way."

Mr. Tony may not yet realize one ironic benefit of his failing eyesight. He requires people to converse, demands them to practice an art form that captures the full attention of his audience. It's a skill that is tangible, important, and intimate. Mr. Tony is still in control.

Age hasn't injured Mr. Tony's spirit. It may have honed a sharper edge to his humor, or brought out a softer side of his competitive nature, but his confident demeanor and youthful gait are still intact. Mr. Tony pays attention, a trait insuring that he doesn't miss a trick.

"This book is my children's idea. I guess it's OK with me," Mr. Tony simply states. "Where do you want to start?"

And we began walking the graceful serpentine path that is Mr. Tony's sweet life.

Frank, Tony and John Rane in Greenbush.

Joseph and Concetta Rane taught lessons of honesty, integrity and accountability, of love of God, country and family. These lessons are being passed down to Rane children to this day and are the most valuable gifts they will ever receive.

CHAPTER 2

Cammarata, Province of Agrigento, Sicily, Italy, 1907

"Con nulla non si fa nulla."
– From nothing comes nothing.

Cammarata, a small village whose ancient structures appear to be carved out of the mountainside, clings to a steep crag thirty miles inland of the Sicilian coast. Surrounded by complex forestland, rich meadows and wide vistas, the area fascinates biologists because of its diverse flora and fauna. A picture of beauty in the early 1900s, the little town of Cammarata afforded its children a natural playground complete with ancient Greek ruins to help fuel the imagination. However, men in Cammarata struggled to feed their families, as the village was poor and people were starving.

This beautiful, but sad environment prompted Giuseppe Reina to understand that the world did not end at the sea, that he could indeed escape the local drudgery of working in the Muti-Coffari salt mine or farming the same land his ancestors had for hundreds of years, and that his desire to see the New World up close could only be limited by his lack of ability to create that vision for himself and his young family – an unacceptable option for a man with itchy feet and a head full of ideas about life in general.

Concetta Reina in Italy.

Imagine a young man walking in the quiet of the woods, talking to himself, practicing the conversation he would have with his wife. "Concetta, my love, we are required to provide our children with a life better than our own. We cannot survive if we stay here. We have an opportunity to build a new world for our family. I want to go to America." Could he say that out loud? How would she respond?

Imagine a young woman with two small children, living in a place rich with history and home to generations of her ancestors, making a decision to uproot and travel by boat to a country she has only seen on a penny postcard. "Giuseppe, I am your wife. If this is the life you envision for your family, we will be happy. I trust in you."

Perhaps there was a longer discussion, a conversation that lasted years. Giuseppe and Concetta grew up together; it's easy to imagine that they fell in love as children, played in the same ancient Greek temple and had their first kiss under the shadows of giant columns when they were seven years old. Perhaps their dreams were filled with travel, and at night their spirits joined hands and soared around the world together. Imagine if they mapped the plan for their lives as children. Could it have happened?

One thing was clear: other men left before Giuseppe and successfully made their way to America. These pioneers sent money and information back to Cammarata, inspiring in their fellow Italian friends great excitement for a brighter future. Giuseppe had to follow.

As a loving couple, Concetta and Giuseppe made a decision that would be a logistical and emotional challenge for many years to come, a decision that would throw most modern-day couples into a tailspin of analytical angst: Giuseppe Reina would go to America alone and grow roots, then his family would follow when he succeeded in establishing a life better than the one he was leaving behind. The journey began.

Giuseppe Reina (left) on arrival in Madison, WI, 1907, with Italian friends.

CHAPTER 3

The Trip to Ellis Island, Spring 1907

Twenty-nine-year-old Giuseppe Reina boards the passenger ship Liguria in Naples, Campania, Italy, leaving his wife Concetta, three-year-old son Sam, and infant son James in Cammarata, Sicily. Giuseppe is in the company of hundreds of young Italian men seeking the same dream, and their excitement, their adrenaline, is palpable, flooding the boat with high spirits and goodwill.

The parting is bittersweet, but Concetta's faith in her husband provides the strength she needs as a twenty-three-year-old young woman raising two children alone. Perhaps she walks Sam and James to the ruins and introduces them to all the secrets of their father's youth; perhaps she frequently

"Bisogna navigare secondo il vento."
– As the wind blows, you must set your sail.

reminds them of their father's love for his family and talks of the day they will join him in America. Almost six years will pass before that day arrives.

Giuseppe travels light as he leaves Sicily, carrying with him two celluloid pins decorated with pictures of his beloved wife and his oldest son, his ceramic wine jug, a few clothes, his knapsack, and his passport. Reaching the Liguria, the ship that would transport him to America, is a feat in itself, involving foot and donkey travel over narrow mountain trails and finding passage across the Straits of Messina. There is no documentation, no accounting for the number of days and the different hardships Giuseppe encounters along the way, but his buoyant spirit leads him on a quest, and only death could prevent his passage.

Giuseppe's passport is his prize possession. It is his ticket to a better life for

The Liguria
Built by G. Ansaldo & Company, Sestri Ponente, Italy, 1901. 5,127 gross tons: 403 (bp) feet long: 46 feet wide. Steam triple expansion, triple engine, single screw. Service speed: 14 knots. 1,250 passengers (56 first class, 1,194 third class).

Giuseppe Reina's passport is almost 100 years old and means as much to Mr. Tony today as it did to his father in 1906. The value of this document to the Rane family is not measured in gold, but in the blood, sweat and tears shed by their brave and visionary ancestor.

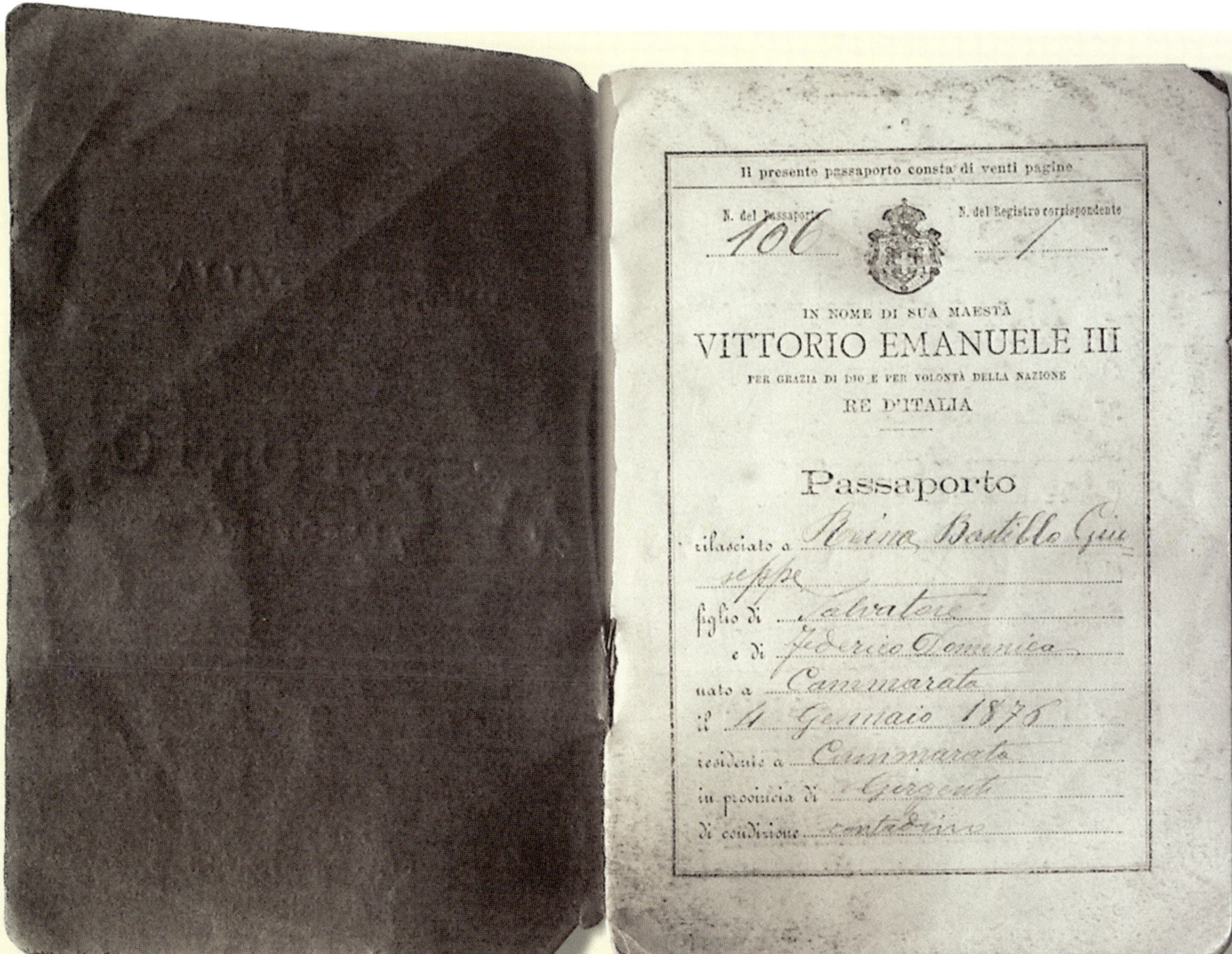

Il presente passaporto consta di venti pagine

N. del Passaporto **106**   N. del Registro corrispondente

IN NOME DI SUA MAESTÀ
VITTORIO EMANUELE III
PER GRAZIA DI DIO E PER VOLONTÀ DELLA NAZIONE
RE D'ITALIA

Passaporto

rilasciato a *Strina Bastillo Giuseppe*

figlio di *Salvatore*

e di *Federico Domenica*

nato a *Cammarata*

il *11 Gennaio 1875*

residente a *Cammarata*

in provincia di *Girgenti*

di condizione *contadino*

himself, his wife and his two young sons. However, the voyage to America is brutal. A steerage pass costs $7.50 and guarantees Guiseppe nothing but a spot for his two feet to stand on and perhaps, if he's lucky, a small metal berth with a canvas mattress stuffed with hay or seaweed. The passengers don't complain about the cold, as the body heat generated by hundreds of steerage passengers is stifling, as is the smell of every body odor imaginable. Blankets are strung down the middle of the large cabin dividing men and women to help create a modicum of privacy. Each passenger is given a tin pail and utensils, and meals are often served from a huge tank, much as one would imagine pigs are fed. It is a humiliating and difficult way to travel, but conditions are much improved over those before the invention of the steam engine as the trip is shortened from twelve or more weeks to approximately twelve days.

Giuseppe and his fellow passengers are encountering the world for the first time and are exposed to a style of behavior that is as foreign to them as the English language they will soon learn. They are thrown into a whirlwind of confusion with no similarities to the loving, respectful homes they have left behind. The passengers in steerage are considered a step above livestock – their lives are not valued, nor is any thought given to their comfort and basic needs. But Giuseppe and his traveling companions make the best of a bad situation, realizing the goal will be met; the suffering will be worth the end result.

As the Liguria nears Ellis Island, the entry point for all immigrants into the United States, Giuseppe's eyes well up with tears as he gazes at the Statue of Liberty. Her message of hope requires no translation. There is silence aboard the ship as the passengers say a prayer of reverent thanks to God and the Lady for a safe voyage, but as the ship docks, the celebration begins. America!

In a split second, Giuseppe suffers the ultimate dishonor of losing his birth name. The Immigration Officer cannot understand Giuseppe's Italian dialect, and with inconsiderate haste, stamps the papers "Joseph Rane" and tells him to move on. "This was part of the price of entry. It was a high price to pay, one that he and other immigrants struggled with forever and never really got over," says Giuseppe's grandson Jimmy Rane, who heard the story repeated time and time again in his youth. Giuseppe Reina's emotional entrance onto American soil tilled the rich memories his offspring cherish today.

Pictured opposite page is the actual celluloid pins. And this page, the ceramic wine jug – Guiseppe Reina's most cherished possessions.

CHAPTER 4

Festa Italia, Madison, Wisconsin, 2004

"Cuor forte rompe cattiva sorte."

— *Nothing is impossible to a willing heart.*

The Italian Workmen's Club, built in 1922.

The Festa priest sees a Noah's Ark roadside sign as he enters the Madison, Wisconsin, area on Sunday morning, wondering if the sign is meant specifically for him. In the midst of torrential rains, the priest appears with a smile and begins Mass by referring to his audience of twelve who stays dry under the beer tent as the 12 Apostles.

Although the weather drives the numbers down, Sunday's small crowd of diehard Festa participants is blessed with enthusiasm, and before long, the beer tent is filled with laughter and excitement. These Italian Americans (or, according to Mr. Tony, American Italians) are determined to relax and unwind despite the ankle-deep mud, the driving rain, and the unrelenting cold wind. The Italian Workmen's Club, whose clubhouse was built in 1922 by the donated labor of Guiseppe Reina and the other founding members, keeps the tradition and proud heritage of Greenbush alive. These men are key Festa organizers, and their spirit cannot be dampened by a little bad weather.

Festa Italia, Madison, Wisconsin, 2005

One year later rain is again imminent, but the afternoon shower serves only to settle Mr. Tony and family into a large, dry tent housing years of Greenbush history, including a vast array of old photographs. However, the verbal recollections are the most cherished – intangible, flowing, melting years as quickly as the hot sun melts ice cream.

Early Festa Italia, Greenbush.

From the monument on the corner of Park and Regent Streets, near the Madison Medical Center: "The Greenbush 1891 – 1960.

This memorial is dedicated to the memory of those immigrants who settled this area at the turn of the 20th century. The Greenbush site, known as the Triangle area, was a unique neighborhood because of 14

Mr. Tony looks at the images with eagle eyes – he knows how to turn his head in a certain direction and see a subject clearly. He circumvents the inevitable total loss of vision through a practiced maneuver; the man refuses to give up for even a minute. "This guy's gone, that guy's gone, this guy's gone," he says, as he looks at dated black-and-white pictures of childhood playmates. "Let's go look for my family." Mr. Tony doesn't dwell on the death of his generation. He quietly acknowledges his deceased friends and moves on.

There is no chance that Mr. Tony will rest this day. He is a compass, and at each turn his magnetic field pulls in old friends anxious to hug him, greet him with good friendly gossip, trade well-worn jokes. Mr. Tony yells to a vendor, "Hey! Is this the way to Lodi?" "You're in the wrong state," is the laughing response. "Hey, Frank! Is that your younger, better looking brother with you?" asks a gentleman traffic controller. Frank responds with a quick, "That'll be the day!" And the banter continues until Mr. Tony sends up his prayers and finally closes his eyes at the end of a very long and fulfilling day.

Greenbush, early 1900s

Only scattered remnants remain of the Madison, Wisconsin, neighborhood once known as Greenbush, as the culturally rich community was eventually destroyed by urban renewal. But when Joseph Rane arrived in 1907, Greenbush was a thriving haven for immigrants who struggled financially to create a new life for their families, yet brought a wealth of social tradition to share with their neighbors.

New immigrants to Greenbush depended on those who settled before them for help in finding housing, food, and jobs, and to ease the transition of entering a strange land with a confusing language. Everyone understood that when one person was lifted up, and another was lifted up in return, everyone would prosper – a simple concept, but not always manifested, as Joseph found out in a hurry. There were a few who sought to take advantage.

"When my father first came to this country, he was looking for work," says Mr. Tony. "He asked an Italian friend, 'How do I go and ask this man for a job?' The friend – supposedly a friend – told him to go talk to the boss and coached him to say in English, 'Hey Mr. Son of a Bitch, I need a job.'

"My father didn't know the language, so he went to the foreman and said exactly that. He thought he was politely asking the foreman for a job. But the foreman was sharp enough to realize that something was wrong. He asked my father through an interpreter, 'Who told you to ask me that question?' My father pointed out the man. The foreman walked up to him, took the shovel away, said 'You're fired,' handed the shovel to my father and said, 'You're hired.'"

homogenous ethnic groups. The community, rich in culture and social tradition, stood unequaled as a neighborhood of harmony and cooperation. This unusual combination of creeds and cultures was destroyed and dispersed by urban renewal in 1960."

Eugene "Tiny" Urso, a generation removed from the Rane children, grew up across the street from the Rane home. His father, Frank, was one of Tony's closer friends. His grandfather, Tony, owned Westside Palm Garden Tavern, and the Urso family lived above it. "The women of that era were tough ladies," Tiny says, laughing at the memory. "That's what I remember about Mrs. Rane. My parents always told me how wonderful Mrs. Rane was, but they never got on the wrong side of her.

Tony, Mayme, Joseph, Frank and John.

Joseph's first job in America was as a laborer, and he worked tirelessly to make a future for his family and to make ends meet. Life was tough. He didn't live in a rented room, but in a rented 'bed,' which was shared with other men, laborers just as he. To save money, he traded for most everything – food, transportation, even the washing of his clothes. There was no money wasted on frivolous things, or his personal entertainment. All the money was saved so that he could bring his family to America. Finally, he saved enough money to bring his beloved Concetta and two sons to Greenbush in 1912. Imagine. Every week for five years Joseph sent the bulk of his meager earnings to Cammarata, dedicated to the dream of providing a better future for his young family. There are no existing letters or records describing those years when Concetta and Joseph were apart, or of the reunion, but imagine Joseph's struggle in learning the English language and Concetta's strong devotion to and faith in her husband's plan and the boys asking constant questions and the excitement when, at last, the voyage is made and the ship finally docks. Does Sam remember his father? He was three when Giuseppe Reina left, now he is almost nine, and his father has a different name. Little James knows his father only in pictures and stories. Love and patience are the keys that must have opened the world for those two young boys, along with a heavy dose of resilient spirit inherited from their mother. The little family celebrates their good fortune and counts their blessings. A new adventure begins.

Mrs. Rane and the other ladies kept law on that block. They kept us on the straight and narrow."

Concetta Rane

Catherine Tripolin Murray, well-respected and beloved author of "A Taste of Greenbush," searches for the perfect way to describe old Greenbush. "Even though the neighborhood was destroyed, the heartbeat is as strong now as it was in the '30s, the '40s, the '50s," she says. "You would think after three or four generations that there would be a cleansing of certain things. There isn't, but I don't know how much longer it will be going on. The church is gone now, but the clubhouse still stands and that's very lucky. There's just this heartbeat that's indescribable – it's there."

opposite page: Frank Rane and Mr. Tony's reflection is caught against one of their favorite quotes on the Greenbush Monument.

Greg Rane, brother Frank Rane, Mr. Tony and Jimmy Rane.

Details from the Greenbush Monument depicting historic highlights of the time.

"MAYBE WE GOT ALONG SO WELL BECAUSE WE WERE ALL IN THE SAME BOAT, AND THE NAME OF THE BOAT WAS 'POVERTY'."
SIMON MOSS

CHAPTER 5

Abbeville, Alabama, 2004

Mr. Tony's home is as warm as his brown eyes. The rooms are open and inviting, comfortable like a pair of favorite shoes. They are filled with memories, and the walls hum with years of activity, buzz like a contented honeybee hive. There's an audible quality that is almost palpable, due in part to Mr. Tony's voice as he describes pictures he can no longer see clearly with his eyes, but his mind remembers every detail.

"When Libba and I built this house in 1953, she wanted the rooms to be bigger than was normal for the time," Mr. Tony says. "She spent hours looking through magazines to find just the right design. She'd take a page from one magazine, then another, and she designed this house to include furniture that we couldn't afford at the time, but she knew what she was doing. Why build a house with rooms so small that the dining room table can't fit in the dining room?"

Ms. Libba and Mr. Tony have been married for 61 years, long enough to create a collection of memories that would circle the moon a thousand times. They are the visual definition of the term "affair of the heart."

"Today is my 83rd birthday," says Ms. Libba. "I'm meeting my girlfriends for a hand of bridge

Libba and Tony Rane have given their family a living example of what marriage should be. "The most remarkable thing is you never hear them saying they had problems and almost didn't make it," says Angela, Jimmy's wife. "I don't think either one of them has ever thought about the possibility of divorcing. They believe there's nothing they can't work out as long as they do it together."

at ten o'clock, then we'll go have lunch and drink margaritas at my favorite restaurant. I'm driving," she says and smiles winningly. "I've packed a little goodie bag for you. Homemade fig preserves."

When asked what makes figs so good, Ms. Libba easily falls right into the good-natured banter. After briefly discussing bee behavior in relation to the sensuous nature of figs, Ms. Libba, without missing a beat, says, "Everything's better with good sex, isn't it?" She doesn't look a day over sixty and is fitter than most fifty-year-old women. Ms. Libba's a dish. Mr. Tony dotes on her, and the return wears well on both of them. It's love that makes the walls of their elegantly modest home hum like a contented beehive.

Ms. Libba, in 1942, with the 1938 car Mr. Tony won in a craps game.

Mr. Tony on the steps of the Frances Hotel in 1942, with friends Kenneth Malcolm and Charles Vickrey.

HOME COOKED MEALS

CHAPTER 6

Greenbush, 2002

"Ogni cuore ha il suo dolore."

— Every heart has its own ache.

Tantillo's grocery.

Tony Urso's Westside Palm Garden Tavern.

Standing on the sidewalk beside Washington Avenue, now a busy four-lane road, Mr. Tony points out where the house in which he lived as a child stood. He remembers where businesses of every kind did thriving trade. His eyes reflect the sadness his soul feels to find so little left of his neighborhood.

"There was a house on this corner," Mr. Tony says. "Right up there was Tantillo's grocery store. Westside Palm Garden Tavern was right there, across the street from my old house. Over there was the Star Garage, and DiSalvo's grocery store was there. He sold all kinds of Italian foods."

Mr. Tony's childhood haunts have been torn down in the name of progress. If Joseph Rane were alive today, he would not recognize his old neighborhood. At its height, Greenbush was full of lush gardens, producing baskets of tomatoes and other fresh vegetables throughout the growing season. Families relied on their gardens to sustain them, and the vegetables were augmented by foods

Concetta in her backyard tomato garden.

Sister, Mayme.

No one was closer to Tony than his four brothers and his sister. That's how the children were raised at the Rane household. They worked together, played together and prayed together. Only God came before family.

bought at a reasonable price from local vendors who had worked hard to establish a business. It was the smell of homemade tomato sauce that called most children home from playing stickball on the streets at night.

Mr. Tony remembers Dominic Amato's grocery store, right around the corner from his house. "Mr. Amato use to hang Italian sausages out on the front of his store. We would look at those sausages, imagining how good they would taste on a steaming pile of spaghetti, until we could stand it no longer." Tiptoeing quietly, Tony and his friends would grab the sausages and run. Amato pretended not to notice, and a few days later a new batch would be hanging there, waiting to be stolen again. "We would build a fire and roast those sausages out of sight of our mothers. They would have skinned us alive had they known we were stealing. Mr. Amato never told on us, and we never told on ourselves."

If Mr. Amato were still alive, Mr. Tony would, no doubt, send him a check with interest to cover the costs of the precious stolen food, as well as a letter confessing his childhood indiscretions. Mr. Amato must have known that by turning a blind eye, he would teach Mr. Tony and his friends the importance of sharing wealth with others not as fortunate. That unbreakable thread binds the very fabric of Mr. Tony's character.

Tony, Jim, John and little Frank in front of neighborhood grocery store.

Jim Rane

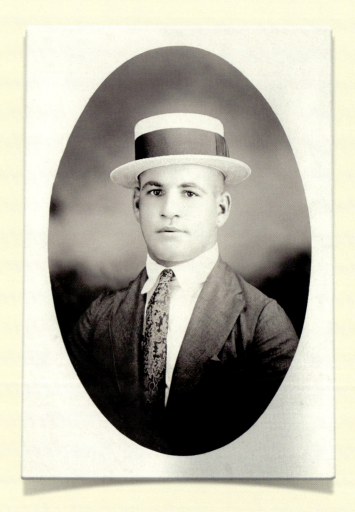

Sam Rane

Frank Rane   John Rane

Greenbush, early 1900s

Concetta Rane built a loving nest for Joseph, Sam and Jim in a small Greenbush apartment at 638 Milton Street. Two more sons were to grace the family at this location – John was born there in 1914, and Tony followed in 1916. It was just a few years later when Joseph and Concetta were able to buy their very own home at 612 Milton, right down the street. Mayme and Frank were born there in 1922. The Rane family was living the American dream.

Neither Joseph nor Concetta had significant formal education. Joseph was a laborer, spending most of his adult years working for the City of Madison. Concetta stayed home to take care of her children, occasionally taking in laundry for male immigrants who lived alone. The Ranes would never be wealthy, but their commitment to their family went far beyond money or material goods.

Little Anthony, Tony to his family, almost didn't make it through the first year of his life. Doctors feared the worst when he developed pneumonia at nine months of age, but even then he showed a fighting spirit and is the patriarch of the family that grew from his parents' love.

"My father earned his living by the sweat of his back," Mr. Tony says. "He built a home, fed us and clothed us. He educated six kids without help or complaint. Never once did he ask for assistance. That's what makes me so proud to be his son.

612 Milton Street, first home of Joseph and Concetta.

Tony, Frank and neighborhood friend pose in the family car in the heart of Greenbush.

The festive wedding of Martino-Mostrella of Greenbush, was attended by Joseph and Concetta (4th row, far right), Jim Rane (back row, 3rd from left), Mayme Rane (2nd row, far right), and John Rane (front row, far right).

"My mom made our clothes and cooked three meals a day. During the summers, I can't tell you how many quarts of tomato sauce she'd put up. That was our staple. Three days a week we'd have spaghetti of some sort that she made with her own tomato paste." Don't bother asking Mr. Tony for the recipe. "It's a family secret and only shared with those who are worthy of the knowledge," says Mr. Tony with a wink and a grin.

Concetta was responsible for the garden, but Mr. Tony picked dandelion greens in nearby Brittingham Park and took them home for his mother to cook. All of the children were expected to contribute to the well-being of the household. Growing up in Greenbush was a lesson in teamwork, in helping your neighbor and yourself. The Rane family was poor, but so were their neighbors. Together they found their way in the land they adopted as their own. Life offered more than learning survival skills, however. Fun was to be had at every turn. A dime would buy a ticket for a Saturday matinee, and swimming was an everyday activity in the summer. The children played baseball in the park when it was warm and played football in the winter, or "the University would flood a field for ice skating, or we'd skate on the lake," Mr. Tony reminisces. "It was a good way to grow up."

Perhaps the words of former Greenbush resident Simon Moss said it best: "Maybe we got along so well because we were all in the same boat, and the name of the boat was poverty."

Tony's brother, John, in front of the family's 1920's car.

Ms. Libba Rane

CHAPTER 7

Abbeville, Alabama, USA, 2004

"Chi incontra buona moglie ha gran fortuna."

— Behind every great man there is a great woman.

Mr. Tony has taken a circuitous route to success. He had no big plan, no specific path. "I don't have a problem with that," Mr. Tony says. "That's what makes life interesting, and a big surprise. I like surprises. My experiences opened up avenues I never even dreamed of."

The biggest and best surprise in Mr. Tony's life has been his wife, Ms. Libba. "If everything was stripped away from me, if an ill wind blew in and took everything, I would be OK because I have the love of my wife and children. Nothing comes between us. Now, I love my grandchildren and my great-grandchildren. But first and foremost is my wife. Then come my children. And then come all the rest.

"It doesn't mean I love one more than the other. I love them all. But you have to remember that when I took a wife, we became one. And that's what had to be."

Mr. Tony will say those words to anyone, in front of everyone, including Ms. Libba. The conversation goes like this:

"Everything I am and hope to be is because of that little girl sitting right beside you," Mr. Tony says.

"Oh my word, Tony," Ms. Libba gushes, with a tad of ladylike impatience harmlessly bouncing off his passionate words.

"I mean it. Listen, I owe a lot to her, because without her, I could never have done any of this stuff. Not any of it."

When asked who's the boss, Ms. Libba doesn't hesitate.

"Tony," she says.

Mr. Tony and Ms. Libba

"But in everyday life, she runs the show," promptly responds Mr. Tony. "There isn't one person who gets to be the boss all the time in marriage."

"Given the chance, I would do it all over again," says Ms. Libba, referring to her love affair with Tony. "Everything, from day one."

"No changes here, either," says Mr. Tony. "I'm so happy."

"It's building your life together," explains Ms. Libba. "It's fun. I know Tony's going to take care of me. Find someone that you can love beyond all else and trust, then marriage is the most wonderful thing in the whole world. People are miserable if they're married and do not trust either themselves or their spouses."

Ms. Libba and Mr. Tony would discuss every move he ever made. "But in the final analysis," Mr. Tony says, "Libba would say, 'Whatever you choose, I'll be right there with you.' I don't care what it was, we would discuss it first, and she would give me her opinion. And some of the time, it wasn't the same as mine."

The decision was always left to Mr. Tony, right or wrong, when it came to business. "About a lot of other things, I would change my mind after hearing Libba's opinion. She's taught

"I told my children just always be honest. Never go to bed mad. Never, never go to bed mad," says Ms. Libba. *"What could it amount to, really? It's wonderful to be happy together, to just sit and talk and not be mad with each other. It works just as well for us now as it did when we were in our twenties."*

me a lot. The Southern way of living is a lot different than the way I grew up. Southerners expound their love more openly. I love the world and everyone in it, but I don't sit here and tell you about it all the time. Libba, and Southerners in general, it seems, are so damn warm. These people down here didn't know me from Adam's housecat and embraced me when I was a soldier. I never wanted to move back up North, so I didn't."

Mr. Tony always felt he could make things better. For himself, his family and others. He says, "My family and I can make a difference in a town this size. It would have been more difficult in a big city, and I know it couldn't be as friendly."

Sometimes it's better to throw small stones in a small pond, as the ripples reach the shore more gently, calmly but actively effecting positive change. And then there are some people who would choose a rogue wave over a gentle ripple. Mr. Tony knows that first hand.

"She was something else, Tony's mom," says Ms. Libba. *"She had this closet in the entrance hall filled with presents. She had a Christmas tree that went to the ceiling. On Christmas Eve, all these people came by her house, and she gave each one of them a present. It was amazing to me! What a generous spirit!"*

Sister Mayme, Tony and Concetta.

CHAPTER 8

Greenbush, early 1900s

"Il fatto non si può disfare."
– What's done cannot be undone.

Greenbush was not all graciousness and good feeling at the turn of the century. Other, more established Madison residents viewed it as a dangerous place. No neighborhood in Madison had a higher crime rate, but not even murder and mayhem could dampen the affection its residents felt for Greenbush. Most who lived there had left dire poverty and deprivation in other countries. For all its problems, Greenbush provided a far better and richer life, a life with more promise, than most immigrants had left in their native countries.

Mr. Tony's walk through Resurrection Cemetery reveals the trouble that Madison residents feared. Anthony Bruno, who owned a pool hall just across the street from the Rane home, was told by gangsters to close shop early one night. He refused, a decision that cost him his life. With most of the Rane family sleeping on the porch nearby, murderers lay in wait for Bruno as he closed his pool hall. The explosion of a sawed-off shotgun jerked the family from sleep.

Not long after Bruno's murder, Antone Navarro, a local grocer, ran afoul of the gangsters. He was shot in the back through a window behind the counter where he worked. Navarro's death hit Greenbush particularly hard. He was a kind man and more educated than most of his neighbors. Navarro readily offered to help immigrants who struggled with the language and the American culture and was loved by the community.

"Right about that time in that era, bootlegging was at its height," Mr. Tony remembers. "The Mafia, or whoever they were, well, Greenbush is where they hung out. We were never afraid of them, but the people who didn't live in the 'Bush would lock their car doors whenever they came through town. At the time it appeared foolish, but I can see now why they felt that way."

Wisconsin state capitol building, 1917.

Even the most famous mobster of them all, Al Capone, spent time in Greenbush. When the heat was turned up in Chicago, Capone and his entourage would show up in Mr. Tony's neighborhood.

The residents would whisper and point as Capone and his bodyguards walked down the street.

"I saw him several times walking down the street past my house. A handful of people in Greenbush might have been involved in bootlegging, but the average man didn't have a thing to do with those people," says Mr. Tony. "Bootleggers even tried to move in on our house because they thought the second floor would be an ideal place to set up their still. They had the misfortune of being greeted by Mrs. Concetta Rane, who chased them from our home and told them never to return. She told them in no uncertain terms that if anyone made moonshine in the house, it would be her," says Mr. Tony, laughing at the memory. Concetta did not speak much English, but her message translated clearly. Her family was never bothered again.

Years later when Mr. Tony and Ms. Libba drove from Abbeville to Greenbush to visit his mother, they stopped in Illinois to stretch their legs and parked beside a hearse. It was carrying Al Capone's body from Florida to Chicago for burial.

Memories flooded Mr. Tony as his walk through Resurrection Cemetery continued. The markers told the story as he paused quietly before the graves of his parents and his brother, John. Mr. Tony suddenly stopped before the grave of Vincenza Bongiovanni, and a dark memory surfaced, as fresh as the day it happened.

Joseph Rane, who had not yet saved enough money to buy a house, lived with his family in an apartment across the hall from the Bongiovanni family. Jack Bongiovanni owned the apartment house, and Vincenza was his sister.

As guests enjoyed Christmas evening festivities, Mr. Tony's thirty-five-year-old cousin Vincenza left the room frequently to seek solace in the quiet of her apartment. Her husband would quickly follow, and shortly the two would reappear. On the one occasion when he chose not to follow her, Vincenza did not return. The sound of a gunshot silenced the revelers. Vincenza had committed suicide. Mr. Tony was nine years old, and the shot that took her life echoes in his head eighty years later.

Mr. Tony shakes his head and says a silent prayer for Vincenza and all the others who reside in his memories, especially the ones who died too soon. The emotion he feels is evident as his eyes soften and worry lines appear on his expressive face. For the first time, Mr. Tony shows his age.

CHAPTER 9

Abbeville, Alabama, USA, 2004

"Nel vino la verità."

— *In wine, the truth.*

A welcomed interruption brings Mr. Tony back to the present. It's happy hour, a tradition that prompts a trip to the wine cellar, a closet in Mr. Tony and Ms. Libba's utility room.

"Pick out a bottle of anything. I don't care. Some of this wine has been here forever. I'm drinking scotch, but whatever you choose is fine with me." Mr. Tony's wine collection includes a bottle of 1967 vintage Chianti Classico Riserva, and as it's opened, the still wet cork falls apart. "Here, use this," Ms. Libba says, and the rest of the cork easily pops out in one piece with the help of a sharp kitchen tool that is as old as the wine. Maybe it's due in part to the festive atmosphere, but that 1967 Chianti has held its integrity, is supple, soft and earthy, and packs a powerful punch. The happy memories begin again. As many Italians immigrated to America they brought with them the traditions that have been in their families for generations. One of the great traditions is making homemade wine.

"In the fall, at our house and every other Italian house I knew of, you couldn't come in any

Mr. Tony, pictured opposite page, with the original family grape press and grape-masher set up at the renovated Stockyard, becomes animated as he describes the way his father stomped grapes in his hobnail boots.

Detail of the company plate, "The Red Cross Manufacturing Company," of Bluffton, Indiana, who built the grape press.

time of day that there wasn't a bottle of wine on the table," Mr. Tony says. "Even when we were young, my mom would always let us have a glass of wine. She said it was good for us." Joseph never took coffee or tea to work. He took wine for lunch in that original ceramic wine jug, as Concetta wouldn't have it any other way.

"You wouldn't believe the grapes that came in by train," remembers Mr. Tony. "Crates and crates of grapes, hundreds, or maybe thousands – there was always so much excitement about the train's arrival." Mr. Tony is animated by the memories. "It was a ritual in the fall that we helped my father make red wine. He had a big trough in the cellar, and he had hobnail boots that were strictly used for mashing grapes."

Before the process of winemaking began, all of the equipment and grapes were scrubbed and washed. One by one the crates were carried to the cellar, and then Joseph put on his special boots. The whole family joined in the work, but only Joseph stomped the grapes.

Mr. Tony begins to describe the art of winemaking with the passion of a master teacher. "The trough was tilted so the juice would go into a number ten washtub. We'd take all that juice and pulp and pour it into 55-gallon wooden barrels. We'd leave it there until it fermented. My father knew when the time was right. The ones that had fermented like he wanted we'd take out and put in the press. Then just the juice would first go into a tub, then into other wooden barrels.

Frank interjects, "But before he put the juice into the final barrels for aging, Dad would light a stick of sulfur, drop it in the barrel, hold it there for awhile, and it would kill all the bacteria."

Mr. Tony continues his instruction. "He'd leave the barrels open for, I don't know, many days, then we'd seal it with wax and forget about it for at least six months to let it age. When he wanted to test the wine, he'd whittle a small piece of wood, you know, just a twig from a tree, maybe, with his pocket knife; then, with a corkscrew, he would drill a hole in the barrel to allow a little of the wine to dribble into a glass so he could taste it. If it wasn't ready, he'd put the whittled piece of wood back in the hole and continue to let the wine age. But, if he was satisfied with the wine, he'd break off the end of the little piece of wood so it would be flush with the barrel. Then he'd pull out the stopper in the bunghole (a hole in the end of the barrel) and hammer the spigot in its place so the wine would pour easily. If the wine had turned to vinegar, we used it to make our salad dressing. It was never wasted."

Tony and his boys goof around in Greenbush.

"The finished product had a very high alcohol content," Frank recalls. "Sometimes as high as thirty to forty percent. The wine was that strong because of the barrels. See, Pa used to buy the barrels from General Beverage. They were 55-gallon whisky barrels. They'd dump the whiskey out, but the wood was saturated with whiskey. So, our wine was aged by whiskey!

"I don't remember dad stomping the grapes at my age," Frank slyly says. "I remember the boots, but I don't remember him using them."

"I do!" says Mr. Tony. "I remember him hanging onto the rafters."

"Yeah," Frank says, "but you're a lot older than I am. You have fifteen years or better on me! If

I'm lying, I'm dying, and I'm still here.

"In the first place," Frank continues, "Tony doesn't remember. He was out romancing and joyriding all the time. Him and his buddies. I was always next to my mother's apron strings and didn't leave the house too often. Sometimes I think I missed my calling. The older guys would see me and say, 'Jesus Christ, is that you again?' I must have been a priest in a different life."

"Now you know why he's the Grand Dragon at the Elk's Lodge," snickers Mr. Tony. "The exhausted ruler, I mean rooster. Anyone who can tell the tales he does, they want him up there."

Most baby boomers remember watching Lucy and Ethel stomp grapes on television and loved the funny antics of these comediennes as the segment unfolded on small black and white screens in living rooms all across America. The intensity of the process escaped us, but we felt Lucy's joy as she danced in the tub. Winemaking was a social tradition for the Italians of Greenbush. It was work, it was real, and it was joyous!

Tight bonds developed among the young men of Greenbush.

CHAPTER 10

Greenbush, 1920s

"Nessuno è savio d'ogni tempo."
— *No one is wise at all times.*

The church and its religious traditions were ingrained in the Rane family for generations before Joseph and Concetta reached America's shore. To this day, Catholicism and Tony Rane are as inseparable as Adam and Eve. Although Ms. Libba attends the First Baptist Church in Abbeville and Mr. Tony travels several miles to Saint Columba Catholic Church in nearby Dothan, the faith they have in one God is unshakable. Now that Mr. Tony cannot drive due to his failing eyesight, Ms. Libba chauffeurs him to Dothan every Saturday night for Mass. She wouldn't think of having it any other way.

The Greenbush Ranes were loyal and devoted members of St Joseph's Catholic Church, where their children were sent to parochial school. "There was never a mention of college when I was growing up. It was never discussed. Getting us out of high school was as far as my parents were concerned, and they took our education very seriously." Tony was a successful student at St. Joseph's parochial school and later at Madison's Central High School.

Tony, Concetta, sister-in-law Mary and friends.

St. Joseph's Church and Parochial School.

Mr. Tony and Ms. Libba have led by example – in their church, in their community, and, most of all, in their family. Their children, their seven grandchildren, and their four great-grandchildren are the focus of their lives now. They love unconditionally and that love is returned.

"The sisters were tough," Mr. Tony says. "They wouldn't think twice about whipping you. If you got a whipping at school, you'd get it again when you got home. I toed the line. My dad said the sisters were close to God. They were representing God, so whatever they said went. If your teacher gave you a whipping, you must have deserved it. There wasn't any sense in trying to talk your way out of it.

"Those sisters made sure you did right. Back then, they didn't worry about somebody suing them or getting their names in the paper because someone's kid got a spanking. They would just take that ruler out of the desk drawer and rap you across the knuckles. It was painful, but effective. We learned not to cross them."

Few of the boys in Greenbush were more popular than young Tony Rane. He was a loyal and trusted friend to many. "He always had a lot of friends," says Tony's brother, Frank, who still lives in Madison. "They were a bunch of dudes. There were two or three different circles of friends in our neighborhood, and the group Tony hung out with had a little more pizzazz. You could always count on them to back you up if you had a problem. They wouldn't desert you."

Mr. Tony and his friends would fight if they were cornered, but they never got into serious trouble. Some of his childhood friends had parents or relatives that were bootleggers or worse, but they all survived their childhood years and deeply cherish the friendships and memories of growing up in Greenbush. "Everything I am started there," says Mr. Tony with pride.

Ann Bruno admired Tony, and she was not alone among Greenbush's teenaged girls. "I remember he always wore a felt hat," says Ann. "I always saw him standing in front of DiSalvo's grocery store on Regent Street. He had a beautiful head of hair, but he always covered it with this hat. My sister and I nicknamed him Topper."

Many neighborhood girls were smitten by the dapper young man who wore the felt hat. "He was the best looking guy in the neighborhood," says Josie Urso, the sister of Tony's childhood friend Frank. "Tony would walk down the street and the Italian girls would whisper, 'Boy, I could go for him.' But our mothers were strict. I used to sit on the porch in the dark and my mother would be downstairs cooking. The boys didn't have anywhere to go, so they would play kick the can in front of our house. My mother would come upstairs and make me go inside. She said, 'They might look at you.'"

Porches were a central feature of houses throughout Greenbush. Air conditioning was unheard of in the 1920s, and porches were not only a haven for social gathering on many summer evenings, but they provided respite from the heat as well. Mr. Tony remembers sleeping on his porch as a child, an option that today would drive imaginative children crazy with

Frank, Butch Oliva and Mr. Tony.

envy, or those less adventuresome grateful for the comfort of an air-conditioned bedroom free of bugs. Maybe it was on one of those hot summer nights that Mr. Tony and his best friends, Frank "Butch" Oliva, Tony Grignano, and Frank Urso, escaped from their sleeping porches and raided a watermelon patch, a favorite pastime of the inseparable quartet. "We would park the car close by and creep into the field, but one night, we got caught," says a smiling Mr. Tony.

The shotgun-wielding owner of the watermelon patch confronted them just as they were hoisting some of the juicy melons, ready to eat and ripe for the picking. They ran for the car and started to drive away, but soon realized they'd left one of their pals behind.

"We saw someone hanging onto the spare tire that was attached to the rear of the car. We stopped the car because we were relieved, thinking it was our friend. But it wasn't. It was the watermelon man, and he still had his shotgun." With adrenaline running high, Grignano grabbed the man's gun and broke it across his knee. "That," says a grinning Mr. Tony, "was crazy!"

Watermelon will never taste as good as the stolen ones from that patch near the 'Bush. And, one may never know if Mr. Tony spoke of his boyhood indiscretions during church confession. That's between Mr. Tony and God. But one can surely believe that a Higher Power protected these boys from their mothers, who would have snatched them up by the ear at the mere mention of a watermelon heist.

CHAPTER II

Abbeville, Alabama, USA, 2004

Mr. Tony's formal education may have stopped after high school, but that didn't stop him from learning more about life, and forgetting more about living, than most people will ever know.

"I was a young boy with Italian parents who set a goal for themselves and their children. Finishing high school was imperative, and it's my own fault that I didn't go to college. The University of Wisconsin was right there." That lack of a college diploma didn't hold Mr. Tony back in his success, but he made sure that both of his boys took a different road than his own.

"My children are very much alike, and they get along beautifully. That old saying about the difference between day and night doesn't hold with my boys. I have two days, no nights.

"When Jimmy was in school, he was playing around a lot. His grades weren't up to par. Libba and I had some bonds we bought during World War II. We sold those bonds and sent him to Marion Military Institute, a good school that helped put him where he was supposed to be. Marion made all the difference in the world, the best money that we ever spent. Jimmy went on to Auburn, then Cumberland for a law degree, then to Harvard. I honestly believe that if we didn't send him to military school, it never would have happened.

Mr. Tony graduates – June 1935.

"If there is any one thing that he has instilled in Jimmy and me, it is that, no matter what you are doing, if you believe in it, never, ever quit," says Greg. *"Quitting is not an option. You may hit a wall and have to make a detour to get around it, but never abandon it. He is staunch about if you start something, you damn well better finish it."*

Jimmy Rane

"It was a different road with Greg. He knew he was going to college and play football. He went out for football at Auburn, but he came to me and said, 'Daddy, I'm gonna have to drop out of football.' I asked, 'Why? You love it so!' He said, 'I can't play football and practice until seven or eight at night and then do homework, too.' Between football and books, Greg's focus was on the books. Of football, books, or playing around, Jimmy would have chosen playing around."

Both Greg and Jimmy have extensive educations, and both went to Harvard and took special business classes that underpinned their natural ability to succeed. The business they own together reflects their drive and dedication. "It's been a joy watching those two boys grow into brilliant businessmen who complement each other," beams Mr. Tony proudly.

Mr. Tony may have limited eyesight, but his inner vision is always clearly illuminated by the sons he lovingly describes as his "two days." There are no college diplomas hanging on his walls, but if the School of Life and Hard Knocks were certified, Mr. Tony would have been an honor student.

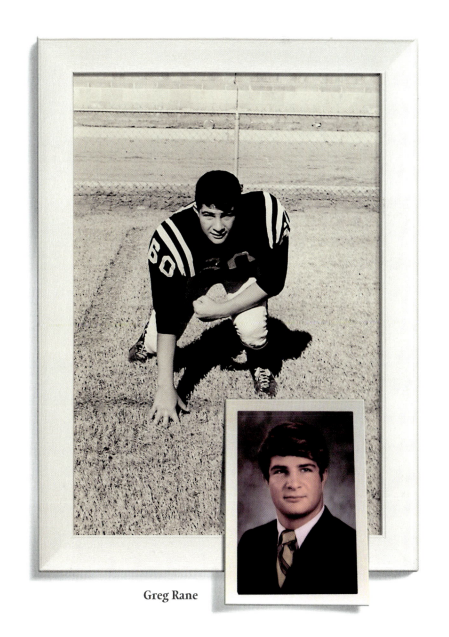

Greg Rane

CHAPTER 12

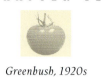

Greenbush, 1920s

"Donne danno, sposo spesa, moglie maglio."

— *The husband reigns, but it is the wife that governs.*

In the Italian way, growing up in Greenbush meant one learned to work hard, to be faithful to God, family and friends, and to respect one's elders. "Our father was loving but demanding, tender but unbending," says brother Frank, five years younger than Mr. Tony. "He was strict as hell with the kids, demanded respect, and got it. He was a typical Italian family man, very compassionate. But he was very passionate, too. He didn't spare the rod. Everybody listened to him. He was in charge. But if one of us was sick, he was so tender.

"He made sure that we went to school and learned what we were supposed to learn the American way. Not many guys in the neighborhood could handle my brothers physically. They were tough. But they knew better than to cross our father. The only person that could make him bend a little

Frank Rane, age one, on the porch of the Ranes' first home, 612 Milton Street.

was our mom. When it came to the house, she ran things. She was the inside boss."

Concetta, a typically busy woman with meals to cook and mouths to feed, a garden to tend and laundry to wash, had little tolerance for foolishness. "The women of that era were tough ladies," Tony says, laughing at the memory. "Our mom and the other women kept law on our block. They kept us on the straight and narrow." Concetta had a unique way of making her point when her children strayed. She would give them a hard whack with her broom.

"The one thing my parents insisted on was that we learn to be American," Mr. Tony says. "The only time we spoke Italian was at home, because my mother and father couldn't speak English well. The more they stayed there and the more they learned, the more English we spoke. They insisted on that. 'If you are here, you are going to be an American,' they would say."

It was all part of the fabric of life in a neighborhood that not many years before had been what most people considered useless marsh land. Italian immigrants came to the United States in great numbers, settling in the area that would become Greenbush because it was land no one else wanted. Soon businesses began

Mayme, John & Tony, 1924.

The Italian Band of Madison gathers on the steps of Wisconsin State Capitol.

to open and succeed. Other ethnic groups moved in. Backyard gardens flourished from nurturing, and so did the neighborhood children.

"We had our problems like anybody else, but we got along," Mr. Tony says. "People helped each other. We respected each other and looked out for each other. If you did something wrong, you were going to hear about it whether it was from your parents or somebody else's parents. It didn't matter whether you were Italian or black or Jewish or whatever. We had no problem with that, really. We were all just Americans. The people in the 'Bush wouldn't argue about just anything, but they would argue over who grew the biggest tomato," laughs Mr. Tony.

"Ogni parola non vuol risposto."
– Not every question deserves an answer.

"There was this amateur night at the Majestic Theatre," Mr. Tony says. "My brother John and I entered the contest. We decided to wear shorts and put on a little bit of a wrestling exhibition. The shorts we bought were loose, and we didn't wear any jockstraps."

As Mr. Tony and his brother performed their skit, laughter rolled through the audience. It grew rapidly louder. "We thought we were doing great," Mr. Tony recalls. "We didn't know what those

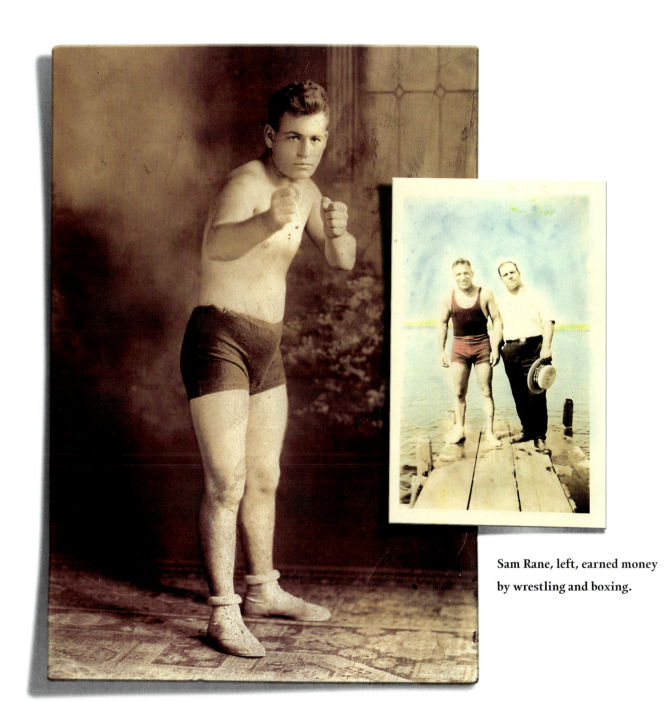

Sam Rane, left, earned money by wrestling and boxing.

people were laughing at. We won five bucks, and that was a big prize in those days."

That experience may have embarrassed Mr. Tony, but not enough to discourage him from performing in front of an audience. As a fifteen year old, Tony was encouraged to enter the Wisconsin state Junior Optimist Club oratorical contest, and he won. A member of the Senior Optimist Club, Mr. Archie Kimbal, and his wife, escorted an enthusiastic Tony to Erie, Pennsylvania, for international competition, where he finished third and was awarded one of his most cherished possessions, the book *Three Points of Honor*. After all these years, Mr. Tony can recite the Optimist's Creed verbatim. "Words to live by," Mr. Tony simply states. "The Optimist Club experience set the tone for my life."

"Tal padre, tal figlio."
– *Like father, like son.*

Mr. Tony's inclination toward hopefulness and confidence infused every step he took on his journey through the Greenbush days. His desire to see more of the world, to experience more than his Greenbush neighborhood, was as strong as his father Joseph's desire to leave Cammarata, Italy, had been twenty-five years earlier.

Family always came first, however. When Mr. Tony was a senior at Central High School, his father Joseph became very ill. A heavy snowstorm blanketed the region, and the inclement weather

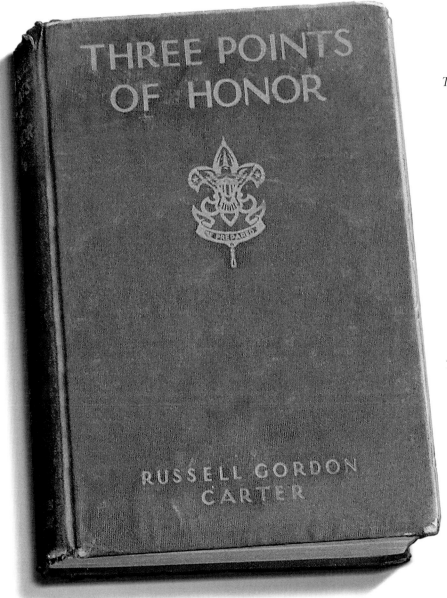

The Optimist Creed
Promise Yourself:

To be so strong that nothing can disturb your peace of mind.

To talk health, happiness and prosperity to every person you meet.

To make all your friends feel that there is something in them.

*To look at the sunny side of everything
and make your optimism come true.*

*To think only of the best, to work only for the best,
and to expect only the best.*

*To be just as enthusiastic about the success of others
as you are about your own.*

*To forget the mistakes of the past and press on
to the greater achievements of the future.*

*To wear a cheerful countenance at all times and
give every living creature you meet a smile.*

*To give so much time to the improvement of yourself
that you have no time to criticize others.*

*To be too large for worry, too noble for anger, too strong for fear,
and too happy to permit the presence of trouble.*

Mr. Tony values his prize book so much that he insists it is "not to go out of this house."

The Central High School yearbook page highlights Mr. Tony among his graduating class.

prevented the family doctor from making a house call. "It was the worst snowstorm Madison had ever had," Mr. Tony solemnly remembers. "Doctor Calucci couldn't make his rounds, so we called Doctor Ganzer, who told my mother to put hot compresses on his stomach. Of course, she did what the doctor told her to do, and my father got worse. We got dad to the hospital and that's when we found out he had appendicitis. The hot applications made his appendix burst.

"I remember the day he died very well. I was at school, and I don't know why, but something,

Divine Intervention, I guess, told me to go home at noon. That was skipping school, and I could have gotten in trouble, but I went home. I was at the hospital when he died that afternoon – John, Mother and I were there. 'Kiss your daddy goodbye,' Mother said. That was March 1, 1935 – a very sad day for all of us."

Jim and John took the responsibility of supporting the family. John convinced the Madison mayor to let him take over his father's job, and he worked for the City of Madison for the next 32 years. Tony helped out by working construction jobs after high school. Tony's brother, Jim, worked for Blieds Office Supply and helped Tony get delivery jobs with them. His most colorful job was with an old fruit peddler who had an old horse and cart. Tony was paid 75 cents a day plus a watermelon. He also worked in the Wisconsin State Capitol cleaning from 3 p.m. to 11 p.m.

Widowed at 51, Concetta devoted herself to her children and their families after Joseph's death. She never considered remarrying. She loved one man, the darling father of her children, until the day she died.

It was 1937 when Tony bade farewell to his family and headed for California. "I wanted to travel," says Mr. Tony. "I wanted to see what life was like in other places." Mr. Tony had inherited his father's itchy feet.

CHAPTER 13

Greenbush, 1937

"La storia si ripete."
— *History repeats itself.*

Out of high school, tired of part-time work, and confident that his mother was in the capable hands of his brothers, Tony Rane was eager to see the world. Back in 1935, one of his first adventures led him to the Madison Orpheum Theatre, where he met Bob Crosby, band leader of the "Bob Crosby Orchestra," and brother of the famed Bing Crosby. The two became quick friends, often hanging out after Bob's gigs and making the rounds to a tavern frequented by University students, kicking back with a cold beer and discussing their mutual love of music. Eventually, Bob became a good enough friend to take advantage of Concetta's homemade spaghetti dinners. Although there wasn't daily contact between the two young men, the friendship was easy and comfortable. A couple years after the initial bond was formed, Tony made a point to run into Bob and his band at the Black Hawk Restaurant in Chicago.

Mr. Tony, never a shy person, told Bob that he wanted to go to Los Angeles and asked him if he could put him in touch with Bing. "Crosby said that it was his father, H.C. Crosby, rather than his brother, who could help me," Mr. Tony recalls.

At the Black Hawk, one could get a whole boiled lobster with drawn butter and julienne potatoes for a buck and a half. Roast prime rib au jus was just $1.90. A filet mignon was two bucks; a pot of coffee, twenty cents. The yellowing menu tells the rest of the story.

"Bob Crosby wrote a note on the menu and handed it back to me," says Mr. Tony. The note read, 'H.C. Crosby, Sr. – 9028 Sunset Blvd. – Hollywood. Dad: Introducing my friend Tony Rane. If you could help him, I would appreciate it. Bob.'

Carrying that treasured menu back to Greenbush, Tony bade farewell to his family and headed for L.A.

Tony and two friends followed Route 66 through eight states all the way to 7th and Broadway in Los Angeles, California, paying ten cents a gallon for gasoline. They

Forty-two years later, Mr. Tony and Bob Crosby renewed their friendship in February 1979. Crosby and his orchestra played at the first Rotary Charity Ball in Dothan, 25 miles from Abbeville.

Courtesy of The Dothan Eagle

Bob Crosby, Tony Rane--And An Old Menu

Sentimental Journey For Abbeville's Rane

Reunion With Crosby

A. J. (Tony) Rane has made the trip from Abbeville to Dothan many times during the years since he adopted the South for his home.

But Saturday night it was a sentimental journey to attend the first annual Rotary Charity Ball.

He came to hear and dance to the Dixieland jazz music of Bob Crosby and his Orchestra. He wanted to see Crosby, shake his hand, and tell him thanks for the umpteenth time.

Forty-two years ago Crosby did Rane a favor he will never forget.

It was 1937. Crosby's band of "Bobcats" was playing at the Black Hawk Restaurant in Chicago — for a lot less money than they made here Saturday night at the biggest event to grace Dothan's social calendar this year.

America was in the depths of the Great Depression. Crosby's appearance at the Black Hawk may have been a very limited stand — but Tony Rane didn't even have a job.

Rane and Crosby became acquainted. Crosby was a guest in Rane's home. They became friends.

One day, before Crosby's band left town, Rane told him he was heading for Hollywood. The bandleader picked up a menu from one of the Black Hawk tables and wrote a personal introduction to his father, H. C. Crosby.

"This will introduce my good friend. . ." The usual sort of thing.

H. C. Crosby was managing the career of Bing Crosby, older brother and one of his seven sons and daughters.

"Well," said Rane, "three days after I showed Bob's Dad that introduction, I had a job working with National Automotive Fiber Co. at Haywood, Calif.

"People just didn't go to Hollywood during the depression and get a job that soon.

"It was one of the greatest favors anybody ever did for me, and I just couldn't pass up another chance to see him."

It's no small wonder that Tony Rane would cherish an old Chicago restaurant's menu, keep it among his souvenirs and bring it to Dothan with him on Saturday night.

Crosby insisted on holding the menu (which held his likeness of 42 years ago) while he stopped playing and Rane stopped dancing long enough for one more picture.

arrived exhausted and aching for sleep. After spending the night in a cheap hotel, they awoke to find the windshield wipers had been stolen off the car.

"Non è tutto oro quello che luccica."
– All that glitters is not gold.

But that incident did nothing to dampen the spirits of Tony and his friends. H.C. Crosby took one look at the note from Bob and found Tony a job working at National Automotive Fiber Company, Maywood, California, for thirty cents an hour. "Three days after I showed Bob's dad that menu, I had a job," says Mr. Tony.

Tony and his friends found an apartment in an Italian neighborhood. It was relatively quiet and they could get eggs, bacon and coffee at a nearby restaurant for sixteen cents a plate. But Tony never felt at home in Hollywood. He had no interest in the movie business; the climate was warm, but the people were not. For an outgoing young man who loved to make new friends, it was an unhappy existence.

"If you were in the movie business, you were King Tut," Mr. Tony remembers. "If you weren't, you were nobody. I decided it wasn't for me." He yearned to move on, and after just four months, Tony sold his 1931 Model A Ford Roadster for $12.88, bought a train ticket to Chicago, and went home, relieved to put the glitz and glitter of Hollywood behind him. Other adventures beckoned.

CHAPTER 14

Abbeville, Alabama, USA, 2004

The phone rings. It's another of Ms. Libba's many admirers wishing her a happy birthday. "I'm going to be late if I don't leave now," says Ms. Libba. "You'll just have to answer the phone. I love you," she says. "I love you, too," Mr. Tony responds. "Do you need any money?" "Let's see what you have in there," Ms. Libba winks as Mr. Tony opens his wallet; she takes a small amount of cash. "Margaritas? I thought you drank daiquiris. You just be careful," he says.

Ms. Libba's body moves with the grace of a cat. "My friends say I drive just like a man. I tell them it's not a bad thing if the man who taught you knew how to drive," she purrs. Her voice oozes honey. She's as smooth as the silk of her blouse, and she's off on her own road trip.

Ms. Libba drives like a bat out of hell. No fear, no hesitation. She is Mistress of the Wheel. "I've had a few speeding tickets in my life, but mostly I've just been stopped and warned," she says matter of factly, as if that's the way it happens for everyone. "One time, Tony was asleep on the passenger side, and I was driving and talking on the phone. Anyway, a state patrolman pulled me over. I remember he had a long neck. We had been to a party, and I thought 'oh oh.' I asked him, 'What are you stopping me for?' He said, 'You went over the yellow line.' Well, I told him I was on the phone talking to my son and told him I must have been dialing then. He said, 'Lady, the next time you want to talk on the phone pull over to the side of the road.'" Ms. Libba takes a breath. She enjoys the telling of a good story and wants to include every detail.

"I started asking him questions like, how long have you been on this job? You're not from around here, are you? How'd you end up way down in this county? Tony was awake by then, punching me, wanting me to shut up. He said, 'No, I'm from Birmingham. This is where they sent me.' I said to him, 'Well, I wasn't doing anything wrong.' And he said, 'Then I won't give you a warning ticket or anything, but from now on, don't talk and drive at the same time.'

"The very next day, I was coming through town, and there he was, sitting in front of a church. And he came and stopped me again. I said, 'What have I done? What do you want now?' He said, 'I just want to tell you that there's a speed limit sign right up the road there. I said, 'I know it.' He said, 'Well, slow down.' I guess he stopped me so he wouldn't have to give me a ticket.

"And then," Ms. Libba continues, gathering speed in the telling of her road stories, "I was late picking up one of the members of the Senior Citizens Club one day. She always stood outside waiting on me, and I was stepping on it. I mean, I was really hitting the road. I was about five miles out, and he was on a side road and came out and stopped me, the same man! I said, 'Now, listen. I know I was going fast, I know I was. But I got this ninety-year-old lady waiting for me to take her to an appointment.' He said, 'If you don't slow down, you won't be taking anybody anywhere!' He got on me good. But he didn't give me a warning ticket or anything. We just had a nice conversation. I see him on occasion. He'll wave to me."

"She's a good driver, really she is," says Mr. Tony softly.

Postcard of Mr. Tony's Long Island, NY residence that he sent to his mother.

New York City, 1939

"Che l'occhio non vede, col cuor crede."

– *Seeing is believing.*

When Tony's old friend Jack Kelleher got a job with a three-piece band playing in the New York City area, he asked Tony to go with him. Jack didn't have to do much convincing. Maybe the East Coast, Tony reasoned, would be more to his liking than the West Coast. And it was.

Tony and Jack went first to Newark, where Tony got a job delivering cosmetics from the Revlon manufacturing plant in Newark to a testing lab in New York City for $2.50 a trip. When Jack's band moved to the Kitty Hawk Bar at LaGuardia Airport, Tony and Jack moved to Jackson Heights. For a music lover, it was close to heaven.

Back in the 1930s, Jackson Heights was beautiful, with rustic row houses and ornate apartment complexes built around spacious, lushly planted interior courtyards. Cappy Lewis, who played first trumpet for Artie Shaw, lived there. So did Gene Schrader, who played piano for the Dukes of Dixieland. Ironically, both Cappy and Gene were from Madison.

The men and women who filled the nights with joyful noise wrote the soundtrack to Mr. Tony's life. Music was a part of almost every occasion, happy or sad, in Greenbush, and a love of music infected Mr. Tony's spirit – so much that he and his friends would perform on stage at the Fox Den, a local tavern. A natural showman, Mr. Tony was the lead singer and loved music and performing in front of a crowd.

"I liked music, but I didn't know the first damned thing about it," Mr. Tony says. "I got to meet a lot of musicians through Jack. Music was my life in New York." Jack eventually landed a coveted job with the famed Tommy Dorsey Orchestra. Even today, Dorsey's orchestra is widely considered one of

The Tommy Dorsey Orchestra.

the greatest dance bands of all time, and featured singers, including Frank Sinatra and The Pied Pipers and Anita Boyer, often took center stage during his shows.

At night, Tony and his friends would go around the corner to Joe Savoia's Bar, where he met some of the most renowned musicians of his time. "After their gigs, the musicians would come in there," Mr. Tony recalls. "Tommy and Jimmy Dorsey, Artie Shaw. They'd all gather around midnight. One guy would pull out his guitar, another his flute. Until about four o'clock in the morning, you'd have the damnedest jam session you ever saw. Those were wonderful times."

Hanging around musicians broadened Tony's horizon in more ways than one. "Marijuana was usually part of the scene," Mr. Tony says. "Sure, I tried it a couple of times. It didn't do anything for me. But I can understand why they smoked it. It seemed to take their music to another level. I'm not suggesting that it's necessary for artistic success, just stating that it was around. That's the end of it."

After working as a waiter at the Schafer Center during the New York World's Fair, a young and enthusiastic Tony Rane landed a job at the Hotel Elysee, a gathering place for the rich and famous on East 54th Street between Madison and Park Avenues. He convinced the hotel owner, who made his fortune selling risqué postcards on 42nd Street, to give him a job as an elevator operator. The hotel's famous Monkey Bar was a hangout for the stars, and the pictures that adorned the walls included

Tyrone Power, Judy Garland, the Duke of Windsor, Rita Hayworth, John Garfield, Maureen O'Sullivan, and Tallulah Bankhead.

It was while working the elevator at night that Tony came to know Miss Bankhead. She stayed at the Elysee while playing Broadway.

"Miss Bankhead would be starving after her show," says Mr. Tony, "and she would call the Stork Club, just around the corner from the Elysee, and order three steak sandwiches. One was for her, one was for the night auditor, and one was for me."

The waiter would bring the sandwiches, but Tony eagerly enforced the house rule that no one other than guests and hotel employees were allowed above the lobby floor. Tony would personally take the sandwich to Miss Bankhead's room.

When she answered his knock with an invitation to come in, Tony would use his passkey to open the door. Sometimes she was scantily dressed, sometimes not dressed at all. "She would holler for me to come in with that husky voice of hers," Mr. Tony remembers. "You might find her in a see-through negligee. You might find her in pajamas. Believe me, she had no

The Stork Club

Tallulah Bankhead

inhibitions. You could see her any way you wanted to."

Talullah Bankhead was not the only uninhibited visitor to the Elysee Hotel. "One time, somebody complained about moaning sounds coming from a room occupied by an Egyptian princess and her English traveling companion. The night manager sent me to the scene – we thought somebody might be hurt. I stood on an ashtray to see through the transom above the door and saw the English woman whipping the princess with a leather strap. The princess was obviously enjoying it," Mr. Tony says.

When most of the hotel food service workers walked off their jobs in a labor dispute with management, Tony saw his chance to learn a different position, to accept more responsibility. It didn't take long for Tony to move up from elevator operator to maitre d' of room service. However, the cook who remained on the job didn't like Tony because he did not side with them in the dispute. "One night shortly after I started the new job, I was waiting to get on the room service elevator. The cook came toward me, and I noticed a napkin sticking straight up out of his chef's jacket pocket. As the cook got closer to me, I saw the point of a knife sticking out. "I just held my thumbs up and said, 'You're the man, you're the man,'" Mr. Tony says. The cook backed off and was later fired.

Anyone with a working knowledge of a hot restaurant kitchen run by a temperamental chef can quickly relate to this stressful scene, and most people would have sought other employment that very minute. Not Tony Rane. His Greenbush background prepared him for all the curves life could throw his way. Well, maybe not all of them.

Known to Elysee guests for getting things just right, Tony's most embarrassing moment involved a wild duck, or at least part of a duck. One of the menu specialties was pressed duck, but the hotel didn't own a press. Instead, Tony would use two silver trays to press the juice out of the roasted duck. The presentation was beautiful, and guests were always impressed.

Tony delivered the room service order to a 14th floor room with a veranda overlooking 54th Street. Tony set up his station on the veranda, taking time to make sure that everything was perfect. He carved the duck and removed the breast, the only part that was served to the guests. He started to press the duck between the two silver trays to remove the juice. But, on this night, Tony pressed too hard. "Whoosh!" he says, gesturing. "That duck went right over the rail."

Regaining his composure, Tony pressed the other part of the duck and served the meat to his unsuspecting guests, who somehow missed the moment of truth between Tony and the breast. He quickly bid farewell and went downstairs, wondering where the rest of the duck had fallen. The laughing doorman walked in carrying the missing meat in his hands.

Life was good in New York City, and adventure waited on every corner for a man with eyes

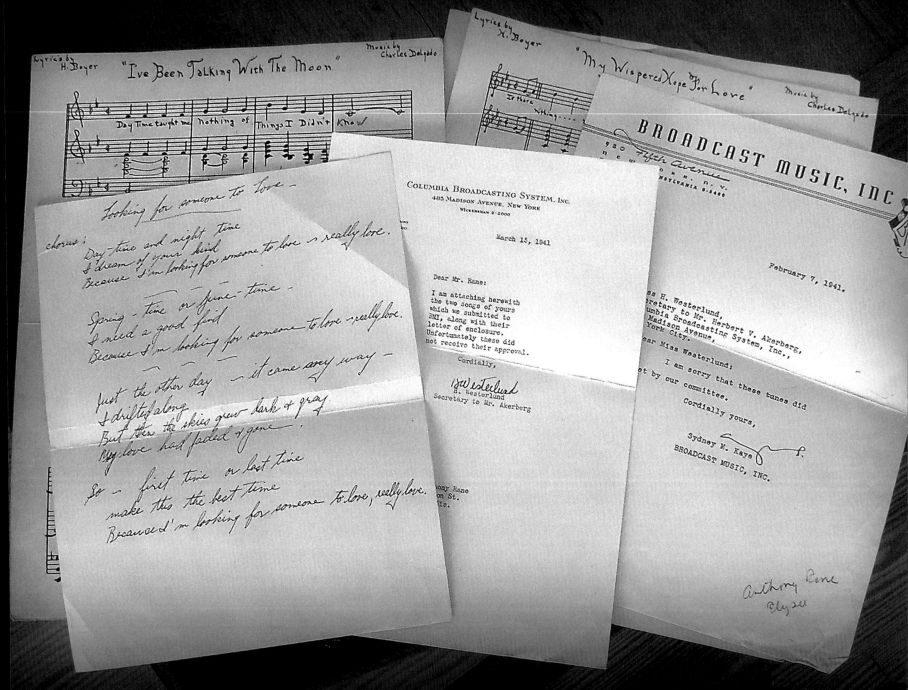

wide open. "I was single and full of curiosity," says Mr. Tony. "There are places I used to go then I wouldn't go to now for all the tea in China. I'm sure there was a lot of crime, but I never noticed it. I could walk down the street and didn't worry about being mugged. You could do anything in New York, eat any kind of food, and meet any kind of person. The people I worked around were actors and big business people (Al Jolson, Ray Collins, Tom Brown), people who inspired me to want to do better than I was doing."

Mr. Tony learned lessons in etiquette and social grace while working in New York that went far beyond his solid home training, valuable lessons that would reappear in his life. Tony's skills in service were honed to a sharp edge, and his natural ease with the world was recognized and respected by the upper echelon of New York society. You have a knack for service or you don't, and Mr. Tony had a knack.

The carefree times would not last, however. Tony was given notice to register for Selective Service in October 1940. He got the call to duty on March 15, 1941. This experience would change his life forever.

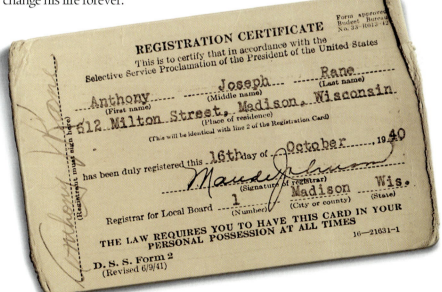

CHAPTER 15

America, 1941

"L'unione fa la forza."

– *In union there is strength.*

Mr. Tony at Camp Croft, South Carolina.

After receiving an extension so he could visit his family in Greenbush, 26-year-old Tony was advised to report to Camp Grant in Rockford, Illinois, on April 15, 1941, where he was inducted into the United States Army for one year of service. Two weeks later, Tony was sent to Camp Croft in Spartanburg, South Carolina, for basic infantry training. Although Europeans were sleeping under a blanket of dark uncertainty, and Hitler had a twisted vision of his own, Americans were peacefully living their dreams. The US had no concept of the destruction about to hit its home soil. "After my basic training, I learned that men were needed in the base hospital Medical Corps. I felt that if I was only going to spend one year in the service, I would prefer to do it in Spartanburg. So I applied and was transferred from infantry to the Medical Corps."

Jim Rane, Tony Rane and Frank Rane

Neither Tony nor any other soldier who had registered for Selective Service knew, at that time, an incident as devastating as Pearl Harbor was part of their future as enlisted men.

Before Pearl Harbor, Tony and his friends would not wear their uniforms when they were on leave, as the locals viewed soldiers warily. However, after the attack on Pearl Harbor, they wouldn't be seen without them. "You'd be considered a ne'er-do-well, a draft dodger, if you didn't have your uniform

Mr. Tony always wanted to look sharp, even during the war. In this letter, Frank is directed to gather some of Mr. Tony's finer clothes. Knowing Frank, he most certainly grumbled through the entire task.

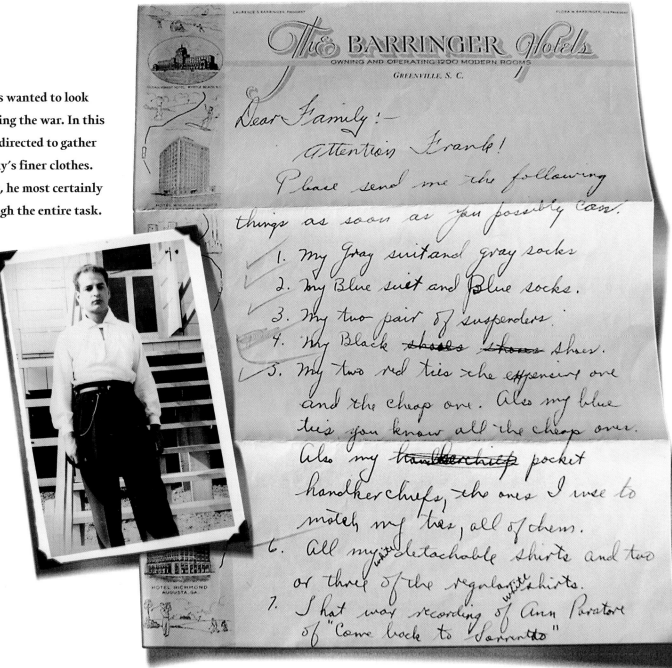

The BARRINGER Hotels
OWNING AND OPERATING 1200 MODERN ROOMS
GREENVILLE, S.C.

Dear Family:—

Attention Frank!

Please send me the following things as soon as you possibly can.

1. My Gray suit and gray socks
2. My Blue suit and blue socks.
3. My two pair of suspenders.
4. My Black ~~shoes~~ ~~shoes~~ shoes.
5. My two red ties the expensive one and the cheap one. Also my blue ties you know all the cheap ones. Also my ~~handkerchief~~ pocket handkerchiefs, the ones I use to match my ties, all of them.
6. All my detachable shirts and two or three of the regular shirts.
7. That war recording of Ann Paratore of "Come back to Sorrento"

on," Mr. Tony says. "After a while, it began to register just how bad this war was for all of us. When we started seeing the movies and learned firsthand how we had been sucker-punched, all we felt was contempt and anger that America had been attacked. Prior to Pearl Harbor, none of us had heard of it or knew where it was. But all that changed on December 7."

Not one person in any branch of the Armed Services knew what to expect. The first few months of WWII were uncertain for every American. Would we be invaded? Could we win this war? What was happening to our country? The men in uniform were as shocked and traumatized by the attack on American soil as every other United States citizen.

Life wasn't easy when World War II began and Mussolini's Italy formed an alliance with Germany. Mr. Tony remembers Concetta's anger at Greenbush Italians who were not sympathetic to the American cause. "My mother, even though she was uneducated and poor, wanted to send money to her people in Italy to do whatever they could to overthrow Mussolini," Mr. Tony says. "There were people in our neighborhood who supported him, and she lowered the boom on every one of them.

"She said, 'You come to this country, you are living better than you ever did and believe in Mussolini? You ought to go back to Italy!' I know she made a lot of people mad, but she was one woman who didn't give two hoots in hell. As long as she believed she was right, she was going to stand up for it. She instilled that attitude in all of us. She may not have been born an American, but she was proud of her adopted country and loyal until the day she died."

Although Tony was satisfied working in the base hospital at Camp Croft, by May 1, 1942, he found himself reassigned and on his way to Ozark, Alabama, and Camp Rucker, one of fifty soldiers who boarded a train in South Carolina and headed south, farther south than he had ever ventured. And once he was there, he hoped he wouldn't be there for long.

"I thought, 'My God, I've come to the end of the world,'" Mr. Tony remembers. "Looking out the windows of the train, I wondered how I'd ended up in such a godforsaken place. All I saw was red

Angela Rane was transfixed as she looked at her father-in-law, a man as strong as any she knew. Tears were rolling down his face.

The Ranes were visiting Pearl Harbor, a trip that son Jimmy had eagerly anticipated making with his father. On this day, before boarding the boat to go to the U.S.S. Arizona Memorial, Angela and Mr. Tony were watching a movie about the sneak Japanese attack on December 7, 1941. Engrossed in the images before him, tears began to roll down Mr. Tony's face. After the movie ended, Mr. Tony quietly removed his handkerchief, wiped his face and filed out with the crowd.

As they boarded the boat to be ferried to the Arizona, lying forever in the watery grave where it sank on that terrible day, Angela softly asked her father-in-law if he was OK. He looked at her and said, "I'm just proud to be an American."

"He made me feel proud, too," remembers Angela. The pride in his country is at the very core of Mr. Tony's character. It's the same loyalty that was instilled in him by his parents after they came to the United States from Sicily in search of a better life. He knows the American Dream. He has lived it.

clay. The stories I'd heard about the South were not flattering."

At Camp Rucker, Tony and his comrades opened a 1,000-bed hospital on May 2, 1942, just one day after boarding the train from South Carolina. "The buildings were built, but there were no soldiers. The minute we arrived, the 81st Wildcat Division began to arrive. Little by little they came. We brought our own drinking water from Ozark and slept on canvas cots, huddled under our GI overcoats at night to keep warm when necessary." Little did Tony know that an angel awaited him, an angel with a majorette's long slim body and a twinkle in her eye that could light up the darkness of a red clay night.

Camp Rucker, August, 1943.

CHAPTER 16

The Red Clay of Alabama

"Batti il ferro quando è caldo."

— *Strike while the iron is hot.*

Libba was a bit of a tomboy, a good baseball player who loved to swing from the boughs of the Alabama pine trees.

Elizabeth "Libba" Mills, a long-legged southern gal with the good looks of a war-time pinup centerfold, told her college friend that she didn't like blind dates, and besides, she had other things to do. But Ruth Richardson was persistent, pleading. Ruth had made a date with Tony Rane, the friendly and nice-looking soldier who worked in the base hospital, but she wanted to go out with a banker that she'd had her eye on for some time, and who had finally made an overture. Finally, Libba gave in. She would do it this once, she told Ruth, but only because of their friendship.

"This banker had been married and his wife had died," Mr. Tony says. "Ruth wanted to go out with him bad. She talked Libba into it, and we got together. I didn't think much about it at the time. She was kind of tall and had spindly legs. I didn't think I'd go out with her again."

But Cupid's arrow found its mark. Tony asked her out again, and again. It wasn't love at first sight between the Catholic-Italian American soldier from Wisconsin and the small town Baptist Irish lass from Abbeville, but as time went by they became inseparable. A love affair began that is still going strong today after more than sixty years.

Ms. Libba grew up in the countryside of Shorterville, Alabama, with three brothers and two sisters. She was the youngest girl and had a natural bent toward playful behavior that is still active today. Libba was quite possibly the most mischievous child ever born in Shorterville. Some people might call that an understatement.

"My oldest sister, Mary Bernice, was spoiled rotten," Ms. Libba remembers. "She always wanted things her way, and we always let her have it. Well, Daddy had this pecan grove on each side of the road. Ed and Robbie and Gene (Libba's siblings) and me would have to pick up pecans after school. Mary Bernice would come home from school and get on Daddy's old gray horse and she'd start down the road.

Mr. Tony and Libba with dear friends,
Charles and Maureen Vickrey, 1942.

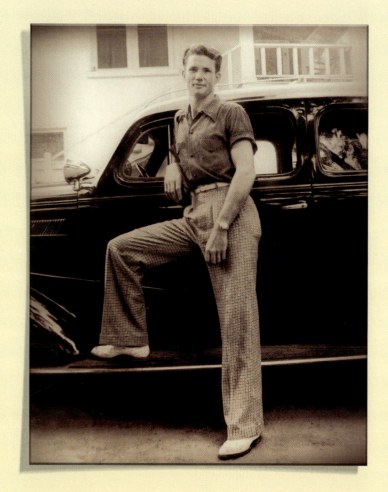

Ed

Gene

"We'd all say to each other 'Look at Mary, she doesn't have to do one thing' and then Ed started throwing pecans at the horse and the horse bucked and threw her off in the ditch. Mama lined us up, and we all got a spanking. I was next to the last one, and waiting for the spanking was worse than the spanking itself."

Libba was a young girl when her father moved the family to Bartow, Florida, during the Depression. "I was too young to realize what was going on," Libba reflects. "I had plenty to eat and plenty to wear and had fun. It was hard for Daddy, though. My brother Bill went to Florida first and found a house and told Daddy he could get a real good job down there. So, off we went."

Ms. Libba's love of driving and breaking rules manifested early. "My older sister Robbie and I pushed the car out of the driveway one Saturday afternoon when Mama and Daddy were asleep. The golf course was right down the street from our house in Bartow. We pushed that car, now, two little girls, neither of us old enough to drive. We pushed it past the house and got in it and went to the golf course. We drove around and around that golf course in the middle of the day. We never got caught. Mama and them never knew it."

It was just a short time later that her mother died. Libba was twelve years old. "It was tough," Ms. Libba quietly states. "We ended up moving back to Alabama so my two aunts, Mary Mills Kirkland

Libba's parents, Lindsay and Anne, with Gene.

and Pearl Mills, could help raise the children. Imagine how tough it was to be a man trying to raise six children by himself."

Libba's father made sure that all of his girls got a good education, including Libba. However, an early school experience with a substitute teacher could have swayed Libba to consider another path. "Mary Bernice went to Troy when she was seventeen or eighteen, and she was teaching by the time I was nine or ten. I remember she was substituting for one of my teachers one day. And I thought, 'Boy, that's good, I can do anything I want to.' So, I sassed her, and she spanked me. That made me so mad that I ran away from school and went home. I hid in the kitchen behind a cabinet and stayed right there. Well, sir, Mary Bernice came home and told Daddy everything. I can hear his feet right now, coming through that dining room into the kitchen. I was so quiet.

"'Elizabeth!' That's what he called me when he was mad. 'I know you're hiding. You come on out of there!' Oh, he spanked me so hard. That's the only time my Daddy ever spanked me. I got two spankings in the same day. I told my Daddy, 'I hate you, I hate you.' I didn't, though. And, I never did anything mean in school again, now, I tell you.

"Daddy said, 'Mary Bernice is a teacher. She is not your sister when she is teaching.' And you know, she was a teacher until the day she died. She got the gene that I didn't. She helped so many of

"I taught Sunday school awhile and I remember the preacher's son and another boy climbed out of the upstairs window," remembers Ms. Libba. "I ran downstairs and called the preacher and said, 'I can't control these boys, and I'm leaving.' I never taught again."

"I loved being a majorette," *says Ms. Libba. "That's all I ever wanted to do."*

Libba's dear friend, Virginia Tiller, 1942.

her students get scholarships. She really believed in education."

Ms. Libba, like her sisters before her, attended Troy State, but she really didn't want to be a teacher. "One thing I really liked about going to Troy State was being a majorette. It gave me the feeling that I was doing something good for myself," says Ms. Libba. "But everybody left school when the war got bad, and we all went to work to support that effort. That pleased me on some level," remembers Ms. Libba.

Libba went looking for work the day the hospital opened at the base, and eventually became Tony's secretary. Virginia Tiller, who still lives in Abbeville, remembers when Libba and Tony began dating. "They just sort of hit it off to begin with," Mrs. Tiller says. "At noon, we had an hour for lunch. They would spend that hour dancing."

A year and a half after that reluctant blind date, Libba agreed to be Tony's wife. But the proposal came after one of the few bumps in their relationship. "He got mad with me about something," Ms. Libba remembers. "It was on Friday and he didn't ask me for a date or say anything about coming over. He waited until we left work and drove behind us. Then he turned off and went toward New Orleans. I cried and cried."

She need not have worried. When Tony returned from New Orleans, they kissed and made up. She agreed to marry, but with the war raging and so much uncertainty, they didn't set a date. Shortly after the proposal, Libba left for a quick trip to Miami to say goodbye to her brother, Gene Mills, an airman about to be shipped overseas. While she was gone, Tony received orders to go to Rome, Georgia, and help open Battey General Hospital. Missing Libba terribly after a ten-day separation, Tony called her. "I know we've talked about it, but do you still think we ought to get married?" "Of course," she answered.

Mr. Tony remembers, "I went to my commanding officer and asked for a three-day pass. 'What for? You just got here,' he said. I told him I was going to get married, and he said 'I'll not give you a pass for that!' Luckily, he was joking." Tony got his pass, climbed into the 1938 Chevrolet Coupe he won in a craps game, and sped to Camp Rucker, where Libba was still working. On September 30th, 1943, Tony and Libba were married at the First Baptist Church in Enterprise, Alabama, just a few miles from Libba's hometown. Not everyone was happy about the union.

"My mother was dead, but my older sister didn't like it one bit because Tony was Italian and he was Catholic and a Yankee to boot," Ms. Libba says. "I told her I was sorry, but I was getting married anyway. Eventually, she grew to love him very much."

The newlyweds returned to Rome and Battey General Hospital, where Libba went to work in Battey's sick and wounded office. The first patients to be treated at the new medical center were soldiers injured at Solerno and Anzio Beachhead in Italy and transported to American hospital facilities

Mr. Tony, 1943.

by train. "They were all wearing the casts that were placed on them at the Italian battalion aid station," Mr. Tony remembers. "Hospital personnel, including Libba and I, were driven to Chattanooga, and we processed those boys on the train so that when we got them back to Battey, there was no waiting for them to get into a ward."

Ms. Libba's eyes well up with tears as war memories flood through her. "Those poor boys," she quietly says. "They'd come in by train missing legs and arms. Some were near death from being blown up, and all we could do was speak softly to them, be gentle with them. It was so hard to watch them suffer." Although shocked by what she saw, Ms. Libba maintained her composure throughout this difficult time. Her soft, genteel nature provided a welcome infusion of comfort to the battle-scarred soldiers.

A near change in destiny happened when, in June 1944, the orders came for Tony. He was being sent to Fort Lewis, Washington, known as the jumping off place for the Pacific Theater. "One day I was with Libba in Rome, and the next day I found out I was leaving for Fort Lewis. We didn't get over three or four days' notice. When you moved back then, you moved quickly. I didn't have time to think.

"I left everything with Libba. And when we said goodbye, we knew there was a possibility of never seeing each other again. We hoped it wouldn't happen, but the possibility was there. We lived from day to day. I prayed that I would see my wife again. The goodbye was heartbreaking, to tell you the truth. It was very dramatic."

Shortly after Tony was deployed to Fort Lewis, Libba developed appendicitis. "I got in the little coupe and drove straight to the hospital and told Captain Todd, my boss, that I was sick," Ms. Libba remembers. "Captain Todd took me to the doctor, and they operated on me that night. He stayed with me through the entire operation." Oftentimes during the war, friends took on the responsibilities of a family member, as that role most often needed duplication. Thank goodness for Captain Todd, as Libba's spinal was not enough to make her comfortable, and the pain was too much for her to bear. "I could feel everything," says Ms. Libba. "It felt like they were pulling my stomach out of my back.

Mr. Tony at Fort Lewis, Washington, with friends.

Captain Todd yelled, 'Stop! Knock her out, she can't stand it anymore,' and that's the last thing I remember. They kept me knocked out for three days."

Tony arrived in Fort Lewis, one of thousands of soldiers facing the next trip out to the front lines, to the action of World War II. However, within two weeks of Tony's arrival, the call went out

Mr. Tony's office wall proudly displays photographs of his officer training class and the graduating class. Photo on this page: Officers Training School, July 1944; and photo on page 107: Officers Training School Graduates, November 1944. (Note the detail photo: Mr. Tony's highlighted himself on the glass of the frame).

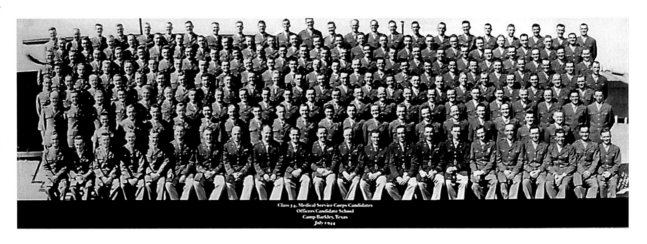

announcing that medical administrative officers were needed. Tony answered the call.

When the Army and all branches of the military begin marshalling and assembling troops, soldiers must go where they are told. Nobody gets to say 'no thank you' to an assignment. Of the tens of thousands of soldiers who were sent to Fort Lewis, approximately 90 percent were deployed to the Japanese Theater. After being at Fort Lewis for a mere two weeks, Mr. Tony responded to the call for medical administrative officers training. Only four people were qualified and accepted from Ft. Lewis. Four people out of thousands. Mr. Tony was one of them. Divine intervention.

Tony was accepted into Class 34 of the Officers Candidate School at Camp Barkley, Texas, where he was stationed from July through November of 1944, enduring seventeen grueling weeks of

Graduates of Class 34, Medical Service Corps
Officers Candidate School
Camp Barkley, Texas
Commissioned 2nd Lieutenants December 1944

training designed to eliminate all but the strongest. Added to this was the strain of being separated from his new bride. Class 34 was a compilation of candidates from all over America. Tony soon discovered that Medical Administrative Officer Candidate School would be one of the greatest challenges of his life. Soldiers were tested mentally and physically day in and day out, and only sleep provided a respite from the stress. With less than two weeks to go, the aspiring officers were to march the platoon in a close order drill. A lieutenant harassed them loudly every step of the way. As Tony waited his turn, he saw one of his comrades get so rattled that he lost control of his platoon, marching them into a ditch. When Tony's turn came, he tuned out the yelling and concentrated on his job. Finally, it was over. One hundred eighty-two candidates entered Class 34 in July 1944. Only fifty graduated. Tony was one of the fifty and was promoted to second lieutenant in the Army Medical Service Corps. "One of the most important things this training taught me was to think quickly," Mr. Tony says. "This is why we were harassed during our training. We had to make snap decisions, and our decisions had to be accurate.

"I learned a lot during the war," Mr. Tony says. "I had to remain optimistic. The glass always had to be half full, not half empty. You lived from day to day because you never knew where you're going. Every day I thought I would be transferred overseas. And every move I made was like starting over."

The job of managing these temporary hospitals to house the wounded and dying was a role that was necessary and deeply depressing. And although his words of optimism are ever present, Mr. Tony's eyes turn a darker brown as he remembers those days.

Abbeville, 2004

Mr. Tony is worried about getting to Mass on time, but he shouldn't as his chauffeur, Ms. Libba, takes the short cut through the Chinese restaurant's parking lot, avoiding a long light. Ms. Libba confidently passes cars that are creeping along at a mere seventy miles per hour in the slow lane; she is talkative, relaxed, and attentive.

"We never know how we touch people," Ms. Libba reflects. "We never know how our actions, although they may seem insignificant, or special for just a moment to us, may have life-changing repercussions for someone else.

"People get so complacent because they have so much. And they forget about other people; they're not close to anyone. Young people today don't seem to ... I don't know ... maybe it takes a war like we went through to make people realize what you're really here for, what life's all about," Ms. Libba continues. "It's about dealing with each other and living with each other and getting along. The world is full of very selfish people today. Things are more important than the people in their lives.

"There's a disconnect between people's hearts and their desires. Their desires don't seem to come from their hearts anymore. Maybe it stems from having too much, you know, not being connected to your heart, and being wasteful."

"Libba, pay attention and drive, honey. You're making me nervous." Ms. Libba doesn't answer, but this is an opportune moment to catch one of her favorite playful responses to Mr. Tony. She may have uttered the words "kiss old butt" under her breath.

CHAPTER 17

Fort Myers, Florida, 1944-1946

"A buona volontà, non manca facoltà."

— *Where there's a will, there's a way.*

Tony received his officer's commission in November 1944. "I was sent to Maxwell Field, which was the Fourth Service Command Headquarters in Montgomery, Alabama," Tony states.

Libba met Tony at Maxwell Field after a long six-month forced separation, and the two took off on a whirlwind trip to Madison, Wisconsin, where Libba visited Tony's mother, Concetta, and the rest of the Rane family. They made the long trip from Alabama to Greenbush, where Concetta quickly and warmly welcomed Libba as a member of the family. It was a memorable experience for a young woman who knew little about life outside the South.

"She was so good to me," Ms. Libba remembers. "She just waited on me hand and foot. I thought she was the most amazing woman. When I got up for breakfast, she always had these great big chocolate doughnuts. Breakfast was the only time she didn't serve wine. I'd never been much of a wine drinker, but at lunch you had to have wine. She said it was good for you."

Concetta Rane left a legacy of a warm and joyous home filled with love, a home offering a sincere welcome to each person who entered its door. It is a legacy that has been passed down through generations of Italian families; it runs naturally and easily and is as deep as Ms. Libba's gracious Southern roots. It is a gift that all cultures recognize, a gift from the heart, and a true heart refuses to deny love based on cultural boundaries. A true heart knows love in every language.

"From Maxwell, I was assigned to Fort Myers, Florida, where I became the Hospital Registrar at Buckingham Army Air Field, a training base for B-17 flight crews," Tony remembers.

"When we first got to Fort Myers," he continues, "we stayed at the Gordon Hotel until we could find a place to live. There weren't that many choices, and as a result, we got to the point that Libba was going to have to go back to Abbeville and live. While I was working, she would scour the town of Fort Myers looking for a place for us to live. She found something, and the man wanted a five-dollar deposit, so if we didn't take it, he didn't lose anything.

"What it amounted to was a very small room, and the door was a half screen door with a piece of cloth tacked over it to give you some privacy. I said, 'Libba, we can't stay here, there's no privacy.'

Tony, Fort Myers, Florida, 1944.

I told the man we wouldn't take it, and he said, 'Well, I can't give you your money back.' I told him to keep it. He needed it more than we did.

"That damn man, he knew we were desperate to stay together. See, Libba wasn't working yet, but she would get a job in the dispensary later. We finally got a room in a nice house with nice people, and things worked out just fine. And then we moved to the Victory Court Apartments and had a dinette, a bedroom and a kitchenette. Very compact."

When Libba tells the story, she says she cried and cried about the five dollars because she thought she had squandered the whole nest egg. "I think she was more worried about having to go back to Abbeville," says Tony, "and I was too. I didn't want her to go back. But, see? It all worked out."

Libba - Ft Myers, Fla

The sacrifices many of his peers made during the war are still vividly imprinted on Mr. Tony's mind today. "I'll never forget the loss of one of our crews. One day, a B-17 crew was on a routine training flight when engine trouble resulted in a terrible, fiery crash. We rushed to the scene but the airplane was almost totally engulfed in flames. We did all we could but the tail-gunner was the only crew member to survive the crash. He died the next morning."

The difficult job of identifying the crew fell to Mr. Tony and his staff. The bodies were burned so badly that dental records had to be used to identify them, bringing home the stark realities of war.

Fortunately, there were opportunities to take their minds off the war.

Haywood Bartlett, from Montgomery, Alabama, was a doctor stationed at Buckingham Army Air Field (BAAF), and he and Tony became fast friends.

Libba and Dr. Bartlett at Buckingham Army Air Field.

On Sundays, Haywood and Tony would go crabbing on the Calloosahatchee River, where Haywood had a house and a boat. "He'd take a string of rope about 200 feet long with stakes on the very ends that went into the ground. About every two feet, there'd be a string hanging down with a piece of fat on it. Then we'd catch the crabs in a net. One time, we caught enough crabs to pick a gallon of fresh crab meat. That's a lot of hard work, but that's what we did with the little spare time we had down there."

The two friends lost touch after the war, but history has a way of repeating itself with Mr. Tony and his family. "One day at The Village Inn he (Dr. Bartlett) walks in!," says Tony. Dr. Bartlett was on a trip to a rose festival in Thomasville, GA, and decided to stop for lunch. He just happened to be coming through Abbeville and just happened to pick The Village Inn. What were the chances? He and Mr. Tony picked up where they left off years before, discussing their BAAF days. "What a special moment. I couldn't believe he just walked in," Tony remembers.

A reporter from the base newspaper Flexigun wrote a small article about the couple although they had been married for over a year. However, their story was newsworthy, and a photograph of Libba as the "Pocket Pinup" was featured alongside the article. The article read in part, "He sang to the beautiful lady pictured to the right and she was powerless to resist. They went straight to the preacher's and were married. (The name of the song is withheld.)"

Maybe sixty years ago the song was kept secret, but not anymore. *Yours Is My Heart Alone*, by Franz Lehar, is the love song Tony crooned to Libba, and he remembers every word today.

For more than sixty years, their commitment to one another has never wavered. The secret, says Ms. Libba, is simple: Love each other, be honest, and don't go to bed angry. The Ranes' blind date bound two young, tender people in a marriage for the ages. When true love resides in the heart, one can have one's cake and eat it, too, knowing there's always going to be more cake. And it helps if the husband can sing.

As the war came to an end, Mr. Tony began to consider his future. He was sent to Truex Field in Madison, Wisconsin, to be separated from the service in January 1946. With his military service at an end, it was time to lay down some roots.

POCKET PINUP

ELIZABETH RANE

After a year and a half of dancing and beach parties and general cutting up, the lieutenant finally played his trump card. He sang. He sang to the beautiful lady pictured above and she was powerless to resist. They went straight to the preacher's and were married. (The name of the song is withheld.)

All this took place at Camp Rucker, Alabama, where Lt. Anthony Rane was working in the sick and wounded department of the station hospital. Elizabeth who lived in Abbeville, a town near the post, was his secretary.

Now the couple is stationed at Buckingham, with the husband working in the sick and wounded office here and the wife working in the dispensary. Lt. Rane entered the Army before Pearl Harbor and got his commission in November 1944.

CHAPTER 18

Abbeville, Alabama, USA, 2004

"A caval donato non si guarda in bocca."

– *Never look a gift horse in the mouth.*

With the war over, Tony and Libba had to decide where to make their life. After weighing their options, it quickly became apparent that Abbeville, the town that had been so good to them both, was the place they wanted to raise their family.

Tony Rane had a lot to learn about being a Southerner. He thought peanuts grew on top of the ground. He'd never heard of sugar cane. But he was a quick learner. He even learned to eat grits.

Life was not easy in postwar Abbeville. The Ranes had lived relatively well on a budget that included Mr. Tony's officer's pay and Ms. Libba's administrative salary. But there was fierce competition for jobs after the war ended. Tony was lucky to land a job jerking sodas for $25 a week at Cash Drugs. "Before I was discharged, between us we were making about $1,000 a month," Mr. Tony remembers. "That was a lot of money back then. I knew I wasn't going back to New York, and I didn't want to go back to my hometown. We were both in love with Abbeville, and if all I could do was jerk sodas, that was what I was going to do."

Tony and Libba struggled to make ends meet. Ms. Frankie Murphy, an Abbeville woman who owned The Frances Hotel and would later offer Tony a business opportunity, befriended the newlyweds. She provided a room for the young couple.

"We really did enjoy living there," Ms. Libba recalls. "We had the run of the whole hotel. It was our little nest. One day, I splurged and went to Sears and bought a table and lamp. I got a lady to make some muslin fabric curtains for us."

When Tony returned home from working that evening, he immediately noticed that something had changed. The new curtains were hanging, and the table and lamp were in front of the window. "People won't believe it," says Mr. Tony, teary eyed at the memory. "That was the most beautiful thing I'd ever seen. We were as happy as could be." Tony and Libba appreciated that one room in the small hotel as if it were a mansion on a hill, although the room they lived in was a converted back

Abbeville's Frances Hotel.

Libba with Jimmy in front of hotel.

porch, and they cooked their meals on a kerosene stove in the hall.

"It was tough when we first came back from the war, but all of our friends had it the same way," remembers Ms. Libba. "No one had anything. We all came home and worked toward making a family. We all basically started from scratch."

Tony knew he couldn't support his wife for long jerking sodas, so his entrepreneurial wheels began to turn. In 1946, he began his first foray into the business world, seeking opportunity and adventure, always adventure. Mr. Tony liked surprises, and his natural business acumen led him down many paths that, while not always smooth or golden, opened doors for his ebullient spirit to glide through, doors wide enough to allow his heart executive access.

His first adventure included his brother-in-law, Ed Mills. Ed and his brother Bill owned a small trucking business called Mills Brothers Trucking, and Tony bought half interest in Ed's truck. A short while later, they had three trucks – an International, a Chevrolet and a White. Their first venture was buying watermelons in Florida and taking them to market. Later they hauled peanut hay that was ground up and mixed with molasses to make feed for cows. They hauled onions from Texas to Atlanta.

Tony and Ed would be gone for weeks at a time, sleeping in the truck. It was a hard life and not the kind Tony envisioned for himself and Libba, who was then pregnant with Jimmy, their first child. Sometimes the money was good, sometimes it wasn't. Sometimes Tony and Ed needed divine intervention to insure a trip was completed.

Once, after picking up a load of watermelons, Ed and Tony ran into trouble. Their truck lost a tire, and they spent most of their money to replace it. There wasn't enough left to buy gasoline, and the watermelons had to make it to a market in Atlanta.

The two men stopped for lunch below Cross City, Florida, at a diner where they could get decent sandwiches for reasonable prices. They talked about selling at least some of the watermelons along the way just to buy gasoline. "It's hard to believe what we went through back then," Ed says. "There were some hard times as far as money was concerned. There just wasn't any."

The diner also had two slot machines. As Tony and Ed headed back to their truck pondering their dilemma, Ed stopped and put his spare change – two nickels – into one of the slot machines. Lights flashed and money poured out. Voila! They had their gas money, made it to Atlanta in

Ed Mills in front of Mills Brothers' first truck.

Business partners Ed Mills and Tony.

time, and sold their melons for a tidy profit.

On another trip, a man out of Chicago told Tony and Ed he would buy their watermelons for thirty cents apiece. Once they were loaded on his truck, the man picked up a brown paper bag and started figuring the total at twenty-five cents apiece. When Tony and Ed confronted him about the difference, the man said they were on his truck and that's all he was going to pay.

"I told him he was going to unload them or I was going to stomp him all over that market," Ed recalls. "The whole market went quiet and everybody was watching us. Then the man wanted to pay us our thirty cents. I told him I wouldn't do business with the likes of him." The man quickly unloaded the watermelons and went on his way.

On one trip to the market, Tony and Ed were offered 75 cents apiece for their watermelons. Tony, figuring that was just the first offer, declined. "We had over 1,000 melons and paid only 35 cents a melon," recalls Mr. Tony. "We had it made, but greed got in the way." The watermelons sat in the sun for three days. The ones on top were ruined by the sun and the rest sold for a quarter apiece, a hard lesson that would serve Tony well in the years ahead. "When you can make a profit," says Mr. Tony, "sell!"

Finally, Tony decided he'd had enough of the trucking business. "My wife was pregnant, I had to stay away from home anywhere from a week to ten days, and it wasn't the life for me," says Tony.

Children changed things for good – and for the better. "Yours was an accident, Greg's was planned," Mr. Tony tells Jimmy amid good-natured laughter. "Tony! Don't tell him that," says a horrified Ms. Libba. "It was just a sweet time," she continues. "Tony wanted six children. He and I both had five siblings, and I guess he just naturally assumed we would have a large family. Well, he married the wrong woman for that! Yes, Jimmy was a surprise, but we couldn't have been happier about it. I'm just glad I didn't get pregnant when Tony was in the service – I needed him close by."

Because family is always first, Mr. Tony was thrilled when Mr. Bruce Flurry, Superintendent of Education in nearby Dothan, Alabama, offered him a position as veteran's coordinator. Tony could work close to home while providing a valuable service to his band of brothers – coordinating their vocational training and expediting their rehabilitation from Army life back to civilian life. But there were many more adventures awaiting Mr. Tony. It wasn't long before the next door opened on his merry path.

Army buddy Joe Klema with Mr. Tony in front of the state office when he was veteran's coordinator.

Tony's experiences started circling back on themselves, although he never planned it that way. "All that New York stuff, working in the Elysee Hotel, in the restaurant, it prepared me for things I just wasn't aware of at the time. But it seemed like a natural fit," Mr. Tony says of his next business venture.

Ms. Frankie Murphy owned the hotel where Tony and Libba lived as newlyweds. The hotel was well-known, and made the national Duncan Hines list of "Places to Stay." She also fed her many customers, serving homegrown vegetables from her tidy garden and free-range chickens that met their demise on her back yard chopping block. However, as she aged, Ms. Murphy realized she wasn't up to handling the daily rigors of running a full service restaurant; her hotel business was doing very well but without a good restaurant that business would decline. Tony saw an opportunity.

Mr. Tony and Ms. Murphy made a deal – she agreed to construct a building attached to her hotel and Mr. Tony would start a restaurant. "Although the building was financed by Ms. Murphy, I had to finance all the equipment," says Mr. Tony. But securing financing for his project became his biggest challenge. "Yes, I had a building, but I didn't have tables or chairs or equipment, and I had no capital. I went to the banker, and I went to a couple of other people who had money, and I couldn't get money from any of them. See, the building was soon to be finished, and I didn't have the first dime to furnish the restaurant. And, of course, I didn't tell Ms. Frankie. She built this building because she knew I would run it.

"My wife's sister-in-law, Mary Crawford Mills, worked in the country for a man named Edward Phillips, who owned a grocery store. Out of the clear blue sky, Mr. Phillips loaned me $4,000. I asked him, 'How do you want me to pay you back?' He said, 'You tell me how you want to pay this back and I'll hold you to it. Make your own deal. I expect you to live up to it.' I'll never forget that man as long as

I live. He loaned me money when nobody else would. In fact, the banker, a year after I opened the restaurant, told me – every Sunday he came for lunch – 'Fellah, you've done a great job. I wouldn't have given you three months to stay in business.' See, he wouldn't loan me money because I didn't have collateral. Can't blame him. It's hard to start a restaurant business and even harder to be successful.

"And then people who had money didn't know me from Adam's housecat, other than I had married a local girl. They didn't have the vision I had of a first-class restaurant. Figured it'd just be another café. I built a canopy over the entrance to my place, and then I had a sign built over it that said restaurant, not café. The canopy idea came from The Elysee Hotel. It just added a certain class. I hired great cooks that knew how to season food. I fixed some of the Italian food, but mostly I stayed out of the kitchen and let the pros handle it."

"That's not true about him staying out of the kitchen," says Jimmy. "He's being modest. That was where he spent his time."

Abbeville had never seen anything like the Village Inn Restaurant when it opened in June 1948. From crisp white tablecloths to soft, indirect lighting to plush booths and waitresses in uniforms, it brought a touch of elegance to a town bustling with postwar exuberance. The food, the service and the atmosphere soon made the Village Inn a favorite stop not only for Abbeville citizens

"Just Before The Feast," Mr. Tony prepares lunch for his fellow Lions Club members. An active member, he helped raise money and gave generously of his time.

but also for salesmen and folks just passing through. Fried shrimp had never been served in Abbeville before Mr. Tony opened his restaurant, and it became a bestseller. Within a year, the Village Inn Restaurant was recommended in a book Duncan Hines published for travelers that listed the best places to eat on the road. "Salesmen lived by that book," Mr. Tony says. "If a salesman was within ten to fifteen miles, he'd detour to our place and eat lunch."

At Abbeville's other restaurants, the owners wore unkempt aprons and customers sat at bare tables on oiled floors. Even the Village Inn's tile floor was impressive, as was the bottomless cup of coffee. Customers could get an entree, three vegetables, a salad and a drink for 85 cents. The other restaurants were cheaper, but the Village Inn was quickly the place to see and be seen in Abbeville, and business boomed.

It was not always easy. Jimmy remembers his father's grace and dignity in difficult times. "As a small boy, I watched him struggle against tremendous obstacles," Jimmy says. "While Abbeville loved mom and dad, there were still difficult situations to be dealt with. But he was just so determined. What I could see in him then was that he would never give up. You could see it in his persona. He would just get more determined."

Jimmy recalls an incident one evening at the Village Inn. There was a party in the private dining room and the public dining room was full as well. "Daddy had called earlier in the day to ask someone to come out and change some light bulbs. No one showed up all day. When the serviceman finally came, it was during the dinner hour and the dining room was full of patrons. The man brought a ladder into the middle of the dining room."

Not wanting to disrupt his business, Mr. Tony told the man to wait until the next day. Tony insisted that he leave, and he did. A short time later, his boss showed up and began to berate Mr. Tony loudly in the dining room. Tony, determined that he wasn't going to have this discussion in the dining room, escorted him out. As he escorted him out, the man turned and swung at him as Jimmy watched, frightened, from a booth. "He swung at Daddy and missed him," Jimmy remembers. "Daddy had done some boxing when he was younger and just kind of popped him, and he went down on the sidewalk. There was a hell of a brouhaha about that."

Even agents of the FBI investigated The Village Inn and found nothing but great food.

Mr. Tony dismisses the talk. But he learned from an early age to stand his ground. A few small situations could not rattle his resolve. He worked long and hard to be successful, and he was not willing to compromise his values in order to fit into a mold that didn't include space big enough for his heart.

Tony took even more abuse when he signed a contract with the Army to feed soldiers, black soldiers and white soldiers. In the early 1950s, blacks and whites rarely ate together in the South. "A big, olive drab bus would stop and unload," Jimmy remembers. "Black and white soldiers would unload. Daddy fed them all. There were those who took issue with that. There was even talk about trying to blackball his restaurant.

"You watch your dad do those kinds of things, and it will instill courage in you. It will encourage you to go against the odds. I watched him do things like that all the time," Jimmy proudly states.

Mr. Tony was committed to making life easier for his restaurant staff, too. When his dessert cook wanted to buy a house for her family, Mr. Tony was there to help. He didn't have enough money to make the loan, so he went to see another businessman and borrowed it. He then loaned the money to her to buy the house. Every Saturday, the cook would make a five-dollar payment to Mr. Tony. When the house was paid for, Mr. Tony went to make the final payment.

"The businessman told him, 'Tony, you don't have to do that. She doesn't know it's paid. You could keep on collecting for years,'" remembers Ms. Libba. "It made Tony very angry. He told that man, 'I didn't know you were that kind of person. She's a very fine woman, and I wouldn't do that to her.' Later, when another dear cook was in the hospital, Tony visited her every day and came up with the money to pay her bill." Mr. Tony gave to others even when he didn't have it to give. Those close to him have seen it in ways big and small. "He'd give his shirt away," says Ms. Libba. "I really don't think he realizes the impact he has on people. I try to tell him sometimes, but he thinks he's never really done anything important."

Ms. Libba is quick to recall an act of kindness that touched her heart deeply. On one icy winter Sunday morning, Ms. Libba looked out the kitchen window of the three-room apartment in which the Ranes then lived. She saw a man, a woman and a boy picking up pecans, cracking them and eating them. The boy was barefooted. Mr. Tony didn't hesitate. He put on his coat and went outside. Within a few minutes, he came back with all three of them. The family was hitchhiking to Columbus, Georgia, and had not eaten in quite awhile. Ms. Libba prepared bacon, eggs, grits and toast. She put the little boy in the bathtub and bathed him. She gave him some of Jimmy's shoes. "I still cry today thinking about that little boy," says Ms. Libba. "I would like to know where he is, that he is OK."

Mr. Tony called Hill Hudgins, who owned Central Drugstore and was the Greyhound Bus agent, and he agreed to meet the family at the station. Tony took them to town, Hill bought them bus tickets, Tony gave them money and they sent them on their way.

See, to Mr. Tony's way of thinking, helping others represents a big piece of the American pie. And doesn't pie taste so much better when it is shared? Sometimes it must have appeared that Mr. Tony gave the biggest piece away, but that's what it means to him to be an American. Mr. Tony recognizes the hunger of others, so without hesitation, he chooses to share his pie; that's why his soul is full and his appetite satisfied. That's why his circle of love is bursting at the seams.

CHAPTER 19

Eufaula, Alabama

"Chi cerca, trova."

— *Seek and ye shall find.*

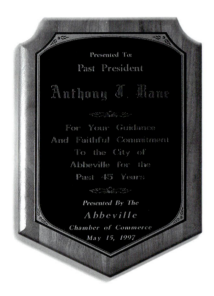

Mr. Tony organized the first Abbeville Chamber of Commerce and was its first president.

As his restaurant flourished, Mr. Tony looked for ways to become involved in his community. Anyone who's ever worked in the food service industry knows how long the days can be. But Mr. Tony didn't count hours. He had visions for his town that are timeless to this day.

In the early 1950s, Mr. Tony joined with other Abbeville business leaders to organize the Abbeville Chamber of Commerce and was elected its first president. The community adopted the hard-working gentleman from the North and began to respect his leadership. "We had a group called the Abbeville Improvement Association, and we invited the Montgomery Chamber of Commerce to come down and help us organize a Chamber of our own," says Mr. Tony.

The Abbeville Improvement Council members sought industry and jobs for their little community. The town was full of veterans coming home after the war willing to work hard to make their town better, veterans starting from scratch. The Improvement Council, the forerunner of the

Chamber of Commerce, was just the right forum for someone with Mr. Tony's natural leadership abilities.

One goal of the group was to get the filling station owners to tell people just traveling through town a little more about Abbeville, encouraging them to stop and at least have lunch or dinner. Highway 431 ran directly through the middle of town and right past all the restaurants. "We designed a brochure, and that was the first attempt to promote the town.

"What else did Abbeville offer then? The Village Inn had been written up in Duncan Hines Travel Guide, you had to pass right by us to get to Panama City Beach. And that's how we first attracted the Pepperell Manufacturing Company to come here," says Mr. Tony.

Mr. Tony tells the story of Pepperell as if he were talking about a member of his family, full of love and emotion and humor. "Mr. Homer Carter, President of Pepperell Manufacturing Company, was passing through Abbeville on his way to his beach house, and he stopped at the Village Inn Restaurant," Mr. Tony remembers. "He liked the Village Inn so he stopped there often. He would ask

Mr. Tony was a founding father of Abbeville's Chamber of Commerce, as well as its first president.

Abbeville is a different town today than it was when Mr. Tony was a young soldier. Most of the businesses that once thrived there have gone, victims of shopping malls and large department stores that draw people to Dothan. But, even now, Mr. Tony's impact is felt. Had he not decided after leaving the Army in 1945 that Abbeville would be his home, the

me questions like 'You've got a nice little town here, haven't you?' I would say, 'Oh, yes sir, we have.' Next time he'd come around, he might ask, 'What kind of water system do you have here?' And of course, I told him, 'We have about a 2,000-foot well that we get good water out of here.

"Was that true? Yeah, well, no, but in my mind it was. The next time he wanted to know about the municipality. I said, 'We have a real young mayor and he's gung ho.' Week after week he'd ask me those questions until finally he wanted to meet the mayor."

In 1951, Pepperell sought to expand one of their plants from Bitterford, Maine, where pillowcases and sheets were made. Mr. Carter was also looking at Cuthbert, Georgia, a small town located close by, but Abbeville ended up being chosen. The plant opened for business in 1953, initially operating downtown in a small warehouse while the plant was being built. "After the plant had been here a year, we had Pepperell Appreciation Day in Abbeville. Since I was still the President of the Chamber, I got to welcome them. That day I helped the entertainment committee with the food by providing my ham. Mr. Carter loved my ham, and that's what we served at his party."

It was a total team effort to recruit Pepperell to Abbeville. Everybody had a role to play and, as a result, men and women were able to get off the farm for the first time, or get out of the house and make a living. They went from working in cotton to making a wage. "We worked hard to get this industry in

Pepperell Appreciation Day in Abbeville, August 5th, 1954. See Mr. Tony on the back row, hand on his forehead prepping for his speech. Pictured left to right: J. E. Dodd, Abbeville Mayor R. H. McSwean, C. S. Keller, Mr. McIntyre – VP of Advertising at Pepperell speaking, Homer Carter, President of Pepperell, Ed Reid of the Montgomery Chamber of Commerce, Ted Ward and Victor Potts.

town's two largest employers might not be there. West Point Pepperell operates in Abbeville, because, long ago, the owner of that company found good service and good people at Mr. Tony's Village Inn Restaurant and decided to establish his business there. Jimmy and Greg Rane, Mr. Tony's two sons, own Great Southern Wood, which was founded by Jimmy in 1970.

Citizens of Abbeville enjoy lunch on the courthouse lawn after the official ceremonies on Pepperell Appreciation Day.

here," says Mr. Tony, "and a couple of years later the union tried to get in. Mr. Carter came to see me and told me, 'If they vote the union in, you are going to have the biggest warehouse you have ever seen.' So, A.C. Richards, R.H. McSwean, J.E. Dodd and I went to everybody we helped get a job and told them, 'Unless you want to go back to chopping cotton for two dollars a day, you better know what you're

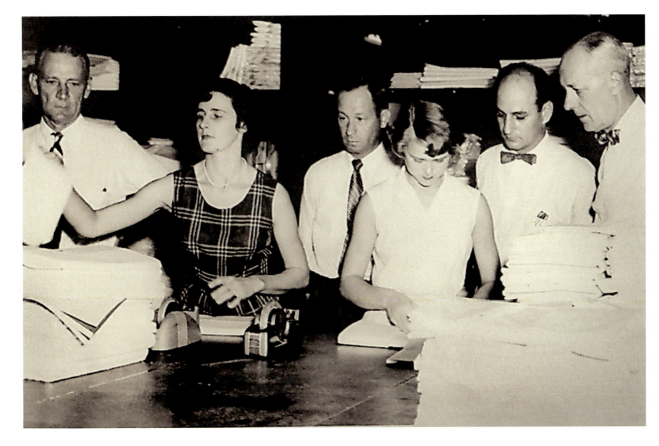

Abbeville Chamber of Commerce visits the Pepperell plant.

doing when the union vote comes up.' As a result, only eight people voted for the union."

Since then, the Pepperell plant has expanded twice, and at one time had over 1,000 employees. Thousands of Abbeville children have benefited because their parents, who a few years earlier were chopping cotton, finally made enough money to send their children to college. Many Abbeville resi-

PEPPERELL

FOUNDED IN 1844

Manufacturing Company

Executive Offices 160 State Street, BOSTON
General Sales Offices 40 Worth Street, NEW YORK CITY

, ME. LINDALE, GA. PEPPERELL, ALA. LEWISTON, ME. FALL RIVER, MA

160 State Street,

President

August 9, 1954

Mr. A. J. Rane
Abbeville
Alabama

Dear Tony:

    Now that I am back home I just want to tell you how good it was to have seen and talked with you last Thursday and to congratulate you on the part you played in that wonderful celebration.

                      Sincerely yours,

                      Allyn B. McIntire

mk

---

dents enjoyed a better life because of the industry that came to town, thanks to the Abbeville Chamber of Commerce, its visionary first members, and its inaugural president, Mr. Tony Rane.

"One of the things we all learned during the war was how much you could accomplish when everyone had a common goal. We had that here in Abbeville," says Mr. Tony sincerely. "It all started with Mr. Homer Carter enjoying lunch at the Village Inn on his way through town. Don't all good ideas start with good food? Without the help of A.C. Richards, R.H. McSwean, J.E. Dodd, just to name a few of many who worked tirelessly, and Mr. Homer Carter, and Pepperell, Abbeville might have turned into a ghost town, like so many little towns within fifty miles of us."

Mr. Tony, one might assume, never slept. He was a member of the Lions Club and served as its President one year. He also served lunch at the Village Inn for the Lions Club's monthly meetings. It was during a meeting when Mr. Tony heard local attorney Forrest Adams speak about the plight of farmers who had to travel all the way to Dothan to market their livestock at auction. Tony's interest was piqued, and, as usual, he didn't hesitate. He and Hugh Herndon, Robert Blalock, and Forrest Adams invested $1,200 each and opened the Henry County Livestock Association. Today, the building is totally renovated and used by the Rane family for special events.

Mr. Tony and Ms. Libba's second child, Greg, was born in 1952, and in 1953 they had finally moved from a small apartment into a home with room, lots of room, and very little furniture. Perhaps this lack of furnishings inspired Mr. Tony to consider his next venture. There were two furniture stores in town, and Mr. Tony thought there was room for another. He sold the Village Inn Restaurant and opened up a furniture store, concentrating his time and energy on his young sons, the livestock auction and his newest venture.

Friday was sales day at the Henry County Livestock Association. Pictured (l to r) are: Hugh Herndon, Mr. Tony and Fred Rhodes at the desk, Mr. J. H. Willaby presenting his stock and Robert Blalock.

In its heyday, the Henry County Livestock Company's auction was a whirlwind of activity. Mr. Tony and his partners were instrumental in removing the burden of travel from local livestock farmers by establishing a first-rate facility in their backyards. "It was exciting," recalls Mr. Tony. "Bulls on one side, heifers on the other, lots of action. The stands were packed with bidders, and it was a successful business venture for everyone." Today, the renovated stockyard is a lovely example of historic preservation and is a jewel in the crown of the pastoral Abbeville countryside.

Hugh Herndon, Robert Blalock and Mr. Tony.

Two successful businesses would be enough for most men, but Tony saw a chance to invest in a product near his home, Fuller's Earth. Fuller's Earth was an ore mined in Faceville, Georgia, just down the road a few hours. Told they could get $32 a ton for the stuff, Mr. Tony and his partners agreed to put up $5,000 each. "We thought this was just gravy," Mr. Tony says. "The hell of it is, we couldn't sell the damned stuff for anywhere near $32 a ton."

The ore had to be dug out of the ground, processed, crushed and bagged. Every Friday, Tony made the trip to Georgia to oversee the operation. Even in 1953 dollars, the profit didn't cover the overhead. In his house, Mr. Tony has a mounted piece of the ore that bears the message, "Lest We Forget." During this trying time, Mr. Tony kicked his two to three pack a day smoking habit! "I ran out of cigarettes," Mr. Tony remembers. "I was going to get some when I went to town for lunch. Something happened and I didn't go to town. I forgot about it until I was ready to go to bed and was going to have that last smoke of the night. I decided I'd wait until the morning. Well, the next morning, I thought maybe I'd see if I could stay off of them. That was October 20, 1953, and I haven't had one since."

Mr. Tony quickly turned away from the Fuller's Earth fiasco and began to focus his energy on building his furniture business. From 1953 to 1962, Rane Furniture Company was the core business that supported Mr. Tony's family. "I got out of the restaurant business because I saw a new opportunity, plus

I really wanted to spend more time at home with Libba and the boys," Mr. Tony explains. "I didn't want them to grow up not knowing their father. It was time for a change.

"Our furniture store was the only one that sold Drexel furniture in town," remembers Mr. Tony proudly. "You had to go to Dothan to Bloomberg's to get it before I opened. Bloomberg's was the place to go. See, they had a furniture store, and they sold dry goods, too. They had it all. We used to call the road to Dothan the Bloomberg Highway. I put a Drexel bedroom suite in my window display, and there was a lady in town who really liked it. Bloomberg sold the same suite for about a hundred dollars more. You know, she went over there and bought it from Bloomberg's so she could say she bought it from there instead of at Rane's, and it was the damn same furniture! That's true!"

Mr. Tony at Rane Furniture Company.

Rane Furniture Company was located on Main Street, right in the heart of Abbeville. The old building was built in 1906 and originally used as a feed store. "It belonged to a man named Mr. C. S. Keller, and in 1953 I rented it from him for $60 a month," says Mr. Tony. "I had to make it look like we were doing a lot of business at the beginning, so me and another fellow that helped me would load the furniture out of the front door, put it on the truck, then drive around town. We would then pull to the back door and unload it back inside. I had to make it look like I was successful because people shop at successful places."

For many years, the furniture store was the hub of activity in downtown Abbeville. It was a warm and friendly place, and all were welcome to drop in. "It was the hangout with lots of activity," Jimmy remembers. "If something was going on with the Chamber or the Lions Club, they'd always hang out in Daddy's store." Mr. Tony put his natural showmanship to good use by working with the Lions Club entertainment committee, and together they established a quartet of likeminded and talented men who raised money for the Club's projects by performing minstrel shows.

Mr. Tony says, "There were some days, though, where we wouldn't sell a thing in that furni-

Rane Furniture Company, on Main Street in Abbeville, 1957.

ture store, wouldn't take in a dime. See, in a grocery store you're selling something all the time, but not in the furniture business. One time there were three days when I didn't take in any money. Then on Saturday, I sold a stove and refrigerator, which made the week.

"Every day, someone would come by to visit. The salesmen would bring these big old books in, like wish books. We sold bicycles, pictures, unique items." Mr. Tony had the kind of merchandise that would stick in a boy's memory. "Daddy had this picture, I've never seen one before or since," Jimmy recalls. "It was electric and you mashed a button and the scenes would be lit from behind. It was plastic and you could change the scenes. You could look at a landscape from out West, or a waterfall, or a snow scene, and you could exchange them, depending on your preference. It was like a shadow box. You could have snow in the summertime and change it to the beach in the wintertime."

Rane's Furniture Company provided Mr. Tony and his family bread and butter for almost ten years, but it also provided a respite from life's stresses for Mr. Tony's friends and his young son Jimmy. "That's just the way it was," says Mr. Tony. "There would be lots of long afternoons filled with lots of people daydreaming. It was peaceful."

One might think that all this business would interfere with Mr. Tony's family life, causing great stress among the family circle. However, it was just the opposite. "We all worked together,"

Mr. Tony put his love for music into action in Abbeville. He and Elbert Tiller sang together in a quartet that put on minstrel shows, singing for community functions and fundraising events. "Tony could sing beautifully," Virginia Tiller, Elbert's wife, says. "He really could. They had a wonderful time together."

remembers Miss Libba. "In fact, one thing that Tony and I both believe is that you should make the most of any situation you're in. Tony spent all those years running the Village Inn – it seemed like everybody in southeast Alabama and southwest Georgia knew him and would come to Abbeville and buy furniture from him. He'd work at the store all day, then would load up the old 1953 Ford truck and go make the deliveries after the store closed. I'd pack a basket full of food and off Jimmy, Greg, Tony and I would go to make the deliveries. I remember it just like it was yesterday. Down the road we'd go signing "Let Me Call You Sweetheart," "When You Wore a Tulip," and "Heart of My Heart." Greg couldn't have been more than one or two years old at the time so I'd make him a pallet on the floor of the truck and he'd sleep through most of the trips. We'd go all over, to Eufaula, Ozark, Headland and Dothan, Alabama, and to Georgetown, Cuthbert, Edison, Ft. Gaines and Blakely, Georgia. We really covered some territory and had a great time doing it!"

I'd live it all over again any day." Mr. Tony echoes his wife's sentiment: "We had a good routine. We just managed it; it was our life! Things fell in line. Libba and I were partners. It didn't seem that we were beating our brains out at all. We had fun!"

About two years into furniture store ownership, Mr. Tony had another great idea. Hugh Herndon, one of Mr. Tony's partners in the livestock auction, owned a grocery store. Hugh sold jewelry in a little corner of the store. "I said to him, 'Why don't we put in a real jewelry store, Hugh? You and I can do it together,'" Mr. Tony remembers. "We didn't know what to call it, but Hugh's other name was Leonard and mine being Tony, well, we combined the two names and called it Lentone."

"Mother and Rena, Hugh's wife, worked in the jewelry store," says Jimmy. "Daddy was at the furniture store, and Hugh was at the grocery store, and both Hugh and Daddy had the livestock auction. It only made sense that this business would be run by the wives."

Lentone Jewelry Store was just up the block from the furniture store, and it didn't take long for it to be blessed by Mr. Tony's good sense and good fortune. The store was very successful and became known for its quality merchandise, including Bulova watches, Lenox China, and other top-of-the-line items, as well as for its friendly and gracious shopkeepers.

Hugh and Mr. Tony recruited Thomas Kirkland as their watch repairman. Kirkland was a parts manager at Baker Motor Company in Eufaula when Mr. Tony and Hugh hired him to work for Lentone. His natural ability to figure out the inner workings of anything, size notwithstanding, was a perfect fit for the budding business. Kirkland was also a lay preacher and according to Mr. Tony, "one of the finest gentlemen I've ever known." Kirkland eventually opened a successful jewelry store of his own, and now his sons have built a very fine jewelry store in Dothan. "The roots continue to grow,"

"In the restaurant business, as long as you are green you're growing, but when you are ripe you are rotten."
Sage words from Mr. Tony.

says Jimmy, "and spread out and affect so many people. A lot of people were helped by the bold initiatives my daddy took. It's lifting people up – it's the American story. When you have good motives, and you work hard, this is the reward. It's this little story multiplied millions of times all over America."

As it turns out, Mr. Tony wasn't quite finished with the restaurant business. When he found out that Eufaula, a lovely little town just up the road from Abbeville, had passed a law allowing liquor to be sold in restaurants, his interest was piqued. "Coming from up North, there were supper clubs that had a band and one thing or another," reflects Mr. Tony. "I loved the food business and accommodations. I thought, hell, people are the same all over. If it will work up North, why won't it work here?"

Tony, on his way to Eufaula for Mass one Sunday, spotted an old house that he couldn't get out of his mind. With the help of Noel Dowling, a banker friend, Tony applied for and received a Small Business Administration loan. He bought the old house, remodeled it into an elegant restaurant, and The Embers Supper Club was born. Like most of his ventures, it was extraordinarily successful. "If you took your wife out for your anniversary or something, that's where you brought her," Mr. Tony says. "Anytime there was an occasion you wanted to be outstanding, my place was where you went. I had a little bar and good food. That was the social center if you were going to entertain people."

Now, back in Abbeville, remember, Mr. Tony still owned a successful furniture store, a livestock auction that helped support the local farming community, and a jewelry store. "Libba had to work in the jewelry and furniture stores while I made my rounds to the livestock auction and the supper club," Mr. Tony says. "Not one time during any of this did my wife ever complain. She was always at my side, supporting me in whatever I decided to do. If she didn't like it, she never let me know it. The finest move I ever made was marrying Libba."

On a typical day, Mr. Tony would go to the furniture store and stay until three in the afternoon, when he (or Ms. Libba with the children in tow) would leave Abbeville with his three cooks – Rebecca, Sam, and Ophelia – and drive to The Embers Supper Club. They would open for business, put in long hours, then drive back to Abbeville at the end of the night. This was a deliriously hard schedule, as Mr. Tony was running a new supper club in another town, a furniture store, and co-managing the livestock auction. Ms. Libba still had a jewelry store to run, two boys to raise, and a furniture store to take over every afternoon and close every evening.

**Concetta.
Mother to six lovely children and eleven grandchildren, she followed Joseph to the American dream and together, they left behind a living legacy. She died in 1957.**

Cody Crawford, a long-time friend, says it didn't happen by accident. "The main thing about Tony, he was always a hustler," Crawford says. "Boy, he didn't let the grass grow under his feet. When he had the restaurant, he was always active helping and waiting on folks. He's just a go-getter. He was wide-awake and willing to take a chance. He was so darned friendly that you couldn't help but like him."

During these early business years, Ms. Libba's father came to live with the Rane family. Ms. Libba reflects, "Daddy got sick and lived with my brother Ed for awhile. I didn't think Ed's wife should have to look after him, and I really wanted him to come live with me. I loved my daddy so much. And he loved it, just loved my children, and loved our cook Johnnie Mae, who spoiled him with a fresh pound cake, hot out of the oven, once a week. Between that cake and the boys, his life was so rich in his old age," she laughs. "To tell you the truth," says Tony, "he was a good babysitter, and he was good company."

Mr. Lindsay Mills, Libba's dad, stayed with the family for about ten years, and he was with the family when Tony experienced the sudden and unexpected loss of his mother. "I got a phone call from my sister telling me that Mother had suddenly passed away. While I called mother every Sunday night and made frequent trips to Madison to see her, to this day I regret not being at her side that day. I guess there's nothing that can prepare you for the loss of your mother, particularly when it's a sudden loss. There's always a part of you that wanted to be there to tell them that you love them one last time."

Then Tony lost his brother John in 1966 and Lindsay Mills passed on in 1967. All of these beloved family members left behind hearts full of love and wonderful memories. "I tell you, it's life," reiterates Mr. Tony. "We grieved, we sure did, and we moved on. We did what we had to do, and we did it together. None of this put a strain on our family, or on our businesses. It's just what happened."

Four successful businesses, a loving family and a strong community service record would be a big enough bite of the good life for most people. But Mr. Tony just couldn't close his eyes to opportunity. As he prepared to open The Embers Supper Club, he became acquainted with Arthur Walden, who owned a car dealership as well as a Holiday Inn franchise in Ozark, Alabama, a neighboring town. When Tony took his new Embers employees to train at the Holiday Inn, he paid attention. The franchise was growing at a spectacular pace, and the town of Eufaula was fertile territory. "I could see what the hotel business was becoming," says Mr. Tony. "If you carried a baby in your arms, they charged. If you wanted ice, they charged. If you wanted a radio in your room, they charged. Eufaula needed a motel."

Tony and Walden agreed they would build a Holiday Inn in Eufaula as soon as the new high-

The large, green, double-arched Holiday Inn sign distinguished the popular franchise from other hotels and motels. "Back then, it was a beacon," Mr. Tony says. "I was against changing it."

Mayor Marvin Edwards, Gene Parker and Mr. Tony at the ribbon-cutting of his first Holiday Inn, Eufaula, Alabama.

way, then under construction, was opened. However, Walden was turning away business at his motel, and the Holiday Inn headquarters suggested he enlarge his place before building another. "That would have meant a delay," says Mr. Tony. "Being the gentleman he was, Arthur said if I found someone else to join me he would understand."

Tony went to work. He had the Holiday Inn franchise, but no capital. Gene Parker, the Eufaula City Clerk and a member of the Catholic church that Tony attended, offered to introduce Tony to people who could help him.

Mr. Parker introduced Tony to investment bankers Hugh Morrow Jr. and Louis Odess of Birmingham. Both gentlemen signed on, and in 1963, the Eufaula Holiday Inn opened its doors. As a show of appreciation, Tony gave Gene Parker 25% of his stock, making Gene an equal partner with Hugh, Louis and himself.

Mr. Tony saw an opportunity to own a piece of the future and got in on the ground floor. "We were number 350 of the eventual 1,700 Holiday Inns," says Mr. Tony. "You know, there was nothing like it in the early days. We offered free kennels for your dog and free dog food. You could park right in front of your room. I got to know the founders of Holiday Inn, Wallace Johnson and Kemmons Wilson. They were aware of and intimately involved with all of their franchisees back then."

As the years went by, Mr. Tony added Holiday Inn franchises in Greenville and Evergreen, Alabama, and Crestview, Florida, to his holdings. All were very successful because of the well-kept rooms, the first-class service, and the delicious food, a Tony Rane trademark. At least once each week, Tony arrived unannounced at each of the hotels to see firsthand that things were being done in the right way.

"We ran our own restaurants at each Holiday Inn," Mr. Tony proudly says. "I bought every roast and every steak for all four Holiday Inns the entire time I owned them. My Holiday Inn restaurants averaged almost twice the revenue of the other Holiday Inn restaurants. When you can make more on the food than the rooms, you deserve recognition. And boy, we got it!

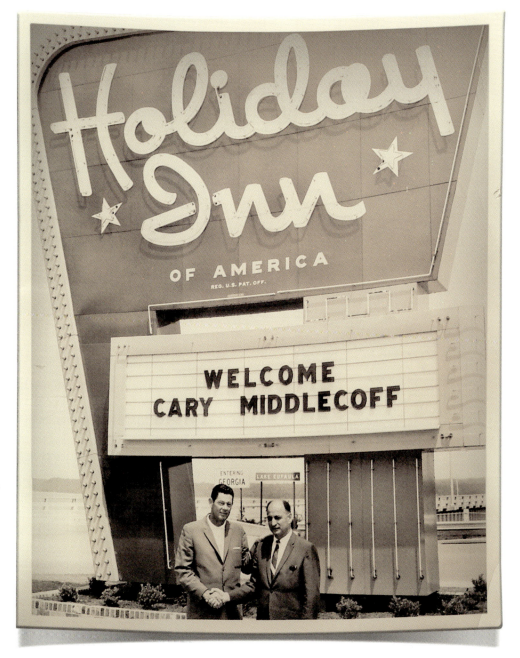

"All this success in the hotel and restaurant business points back to my New York experience working at the Elysee Hotel. I didn't have any idea that I would end up in the business later. Not one bit of an idea. But that's what life's all about. That's what makes it fun," Tony smiles and says.

Mr. Tony served on almost every committee established by the International Association of Holiday Inns, including the Food and Beverage Committee, the Governmental Affairs Committee and the Education Committee. "See, the Association always worked to better the Holiday Inns. The parent company was always working with us, too, but the International Association is the group that promoted a lot of the things that were accomplished. You have to be appointed to serve on their committees; you can't just volunteer. Now, we made some mistakes, but we learned from them. That's the reason that being on these committees was so valuable."

Tom Kelly presenting Mr. Tony the 'Mr. Alabama Travel' award.

One mistake that Mr. Tony remembers centers around his passion for the food industry. "The Food and Beverage Committee decided that each hotel would serve the same menu on Sunday. From Eufaula, Alabama, to New York City, all Holiday Inn restaurants served fried chicken and mashed potatoes family-style. The problem was that the price stayed the same everywhere. Now, I could serve fried chicken down here a lot cheaper than they could in New York, and that's where we made our mistake. It didn't take long for us to figure that one out. That promotion didn't last long."

All things being equal in the world of franchised operations, the two distinctions that separated Mr. Tony's motels from the rest were food and service. His motels became known nationally as some of the finest in the booming Holiday Inn chain, and they consistently finished in the top eight percent, or in the top 100, in the entire world.

Mr. Tony became a big player in the Alabama travel industry and was an active member of the Alabama Travel Council because he believed promoting tourism was crucial for the success of his businesses. During his tenure, Mr. Tony helped promote the building of welcome stations that are now a familiar part of the landscape. This was done in conjunction with the Alabama Bureau of Publicity and Information. In 1978, Mr. Tony was named Mr. Alabama Travel, the most prestigious award given by the Council and inducted into the Alabama Hospitality Hall of Fame.

"I was elected President of the Alabama Travel Council and was president for seven years," says Mr. Tony matter of factly. "We spent all of our time promoting Alabama, making it a destination state rather than a through state to Florida. Every year for ten years we would invite travel agents and travel writers from all over the United States and the world, to come to Montgomery, Alabama. Then for ten days, we'd make a whirlwind tour of the state on a chartered Trailways bus. No other states did this."

All the motel rooms were complimented for the travel industry connections, and their meals

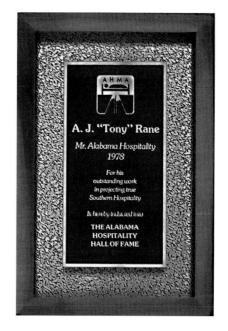

The 'Mr. Alabama Travel' award.

As president of the Alabama Travel Council, Mr. Tony helped position the state as a 'destination' – not just a highway to Florida.

and the nightly cocktail parties were furnished by the local Chamber of Commerce or a civic group. "It didn't cost the travel writers a dime except for their fare to Alabama," says Mr. Tony, "and it was always a big party that paid big dividends."

In the midst of running his Holiday Inns and promoting his adopted state, Mr. Tony found time to serve a seven-year stint as one of 10 members of the State Board of Education's Advisory Council on Vocational Education.

Eventually, Mr. Tony took stock of his work, was satisfied with his business success, and made a decision. In the early '80s, he sold his hotel properties, became an investor and began to relax and enjoy the fruits of his labor. He looks back with the satisfaction of one who knows he had the courage to take chances, to do his level best on any given day, and to get the best out of his employees. "There's an old saying that a 1,000-mile trip starts with the first step," Mr. Tony says. "I saw a need for these things in our town and in our region. I had a lot of success. I was blessed."

Tony often worked long and grueling hours, but he did it with a smile on his face and a song in his heart. And Libba was always there to offer support, to help when asked, and to hold down the home front. "Think about having to go to work for eight to ten hours a day and having to do something you dislike," Mr. Tony says. "Think about being married to somebody you married just for the money and what it would be like to have to be with that person every day. I can't see how somebody could marry a person they didn't love, and I can't imagine how hard it would be to go to work everyday and do something you don't like.

"I appreciate what my wife did in raising those kids. Sometimes, I'd leave early and come back late. I heard a long time ago that if you look after your business, your business will look after you. But I don't care what it was – the restaurant, the nightclub, the livestock, the jewelry store, the hotels – none of it mattered without love."

Mr. Tony knows that, although he has opened and closed more successful businesses than most people have ever dreamed of owning, his greatest and most fulfilling success continues to be Ms. Libba and his boys. He has a passion for life, seizes opportunity by the tail, and brings it in and makes it his regardless of the challenge. The word "no" is not in his vocabulary, nor is the word "boredom." He is an optimist from the top of his head to the tip of his toes and understands the value of commitment. Herein lies the lesson for everyone who reads this book. Mr. Tony is centered, and he knows naturally how to balance head and heart.

Sound simple? Yes, but simple, like Mr. Tony's homemade spaghetti sauce, cannot be defined as easy.

CHAPTER 20

Abbeville, Alabama, USA, 2004

It takes about two minutes to feel like family at Mr. Tony and Ms. Libba's home. The shoes are kicked off, the pillows get rearranged for maximum comfort, and the eyelids fall to half mast.

Southern Living could have learned a few things from Ms. Libba. Her sense of style is as natural as the tall ferns in her back yard, as quietly elegant as the deer that frolic in the Alabama backwoods early in the morning. Everything belongs in the Rane home, and Ms. Libba lets it all fall into place, naturally, with no worry or pretension. She is a natural-born designer, and comfort is her specialty.

"Jimmy never wanted to go to sleep at night when he was younger, so now he comes over to catch up on his naps," Ms. Libba quietly laughs. Jimmy's shoes are off and his eyelids are closed, but he smiles. Big cats never really sleep.

"L'occhio del padrone ingrassa il cavallo."

– *The eye of the owner makes the horse fat.*

Mr. Tony had not agreed with his son's decision to borrow $76,000 from the Bank of Abbeville to start Great Southern Wood in 1970. And in the early years, Mr. Tony's reservations about his son's business decision seemed well founded. Jimmy Rane's fledgling business was struggling to make ends meet. "I was totally against Jimmy buying this wood business," says Mr. Tony. "He had gone to school to be a lawyer, and here he was turning his back on that career. I just couldn't understand it at the time."

"The worst confrontation we ever had was when I bought the business," remembers Jimmy. "Daddy just detached himself emotionally and had no enthusiasm for my decision. It was awful for me. He was totally disengaged. But he helped me get the money I needed by co-signing my loan."

In its infancy, Mr. Tony wouldn't even stop by Jimmy's office at Great Southern. He drove right by the business every day, until finally Jimmy put in a gas pump out front, "primarily to get him to stop," Jimmy says, laughing. "Well, it worked. He'd stop to get gas, but then he'd drive on." Mr. Tony took chances in business with great results, but he just couldn't understand why his son wanted to walk the same path. Jimmy was only doing what came naturally to him, however. Following his heart in business was his birthright.

"I was a junior in law school at Cumberland in May 1970," Jimmy says. "In June of that same year, my first wife's parents were killed in a car wreck. Mr. Roberts, my father-in-law at the time, owned a small wood business where he made fence posts. At the time of his death in 1970, the US inheritance tax law allowed each estate a $60,000 exemption. The entire estate over $60,000 was then taxed at 55%. Like many landowners in the South at that time, Mr. Roberts' assets were largely tied up in his land. If the government valued the land at a high price, it would be impossible to pay the inheritance tax. Therefore, on the advice of Mr. E. B. McDaniel, the CPA who was handling the Roberts estate, the decision was taken not to sell any real estate but to convert all the personal property to cash in order to pay the inheritance taxes."

How to turn a small, backyard fence post manufacturing plant into cash was Jimmy's charge. At first, he tried to sell it. All the family members didn't agree on this strategy and disagreements were brewing. The estate had received just one offer to purchase the wood preserving plant. It was from Ralph Reynolds and was for $14,000 including the land. In order to adhere to the advice of Mr. McDaniel, Jimmy crafted a solution. He would offer to purchase the equipment and lease the land.

"I saw a letter from Osmose Wood Preserving in Mr. Roberts' office," Jimmy said. "I didn't know who they were, but called the company for advice. I asked, 'How do I get rid of this equipment?' I was told, 'First you have to fix it because it's all broken.' That's when I decided to offer to buy the equipment for $10,000 and lease the land for $4,000 a year," Jimmy recalls. "Daddy and I argued bitterly over this decision. He couldn't believe I had spent all this time going to school to be an attorney

The first year Great Southern Wood was in business (1971), total sales were $22,000. Last year sales were over a half billion. Yep. That's billion, with a B. Today, Great Southern is recognized by *Building Products Digest* as the second largest treater in the industry with eight treating plants and a distribution area covering a 12 state region in the Southern United States.

Jimmy on the balcony of the Ilikai Hotel, September, 1970.

and was turning my back on my education." Even though their relationship was strained, Mr. Tony helped Jimmy borrow $76,000 to repair and refurbish the plant.

Jimmy had been offered a job with the law firm Baker, McDaniel & Hall in Birmingham, and he wanted to accept it. However, the Roberts estate was still unsettled, and the wood business needed immediate attention. Once again, Jimmy crafted a solution. He decided to take on a partner.

A close friend, Phillip McMahon from Birmingham, was serving his country in Vietnam and was due for a period of rest and relaxation in Honolulu, Hawaii, in September 1970. In a bold move, Jimmy decided to go to Hawaii to pitch Phillip on becoming his partner in the business. He flew to Honolulu to meet with Phillip and his wife, Sandra, for several days. Phillip's tour of duty was to end in mid-November, and he was planning to return to Birmingham, but he didn't have a job waiting on him. The two men agreed to go into business together. When Phillip returned home from Vietnam, he and Sandra moved to Abbeville where Phillip immediately began to oversee the reconstruction and renovation of the plant. By April 1971, they were ready to open.

Jimmy would come home from Birmingham on the weekends and help until he graduated in May, then spent a grueling summer working at the plant while at the same time studying for the bar exam which he took in July. Before he heard the results of his bar exam, Phillip decided he had had enough and wanted to return to Birmingham. Mr. Tony graciously bought him out.

It was now September 1971, and Jimmy had just passed the bar exam.

Still dreaming of being an attorney, he opened a one-room, one-man law practice in downtown Abbeville, but every morning he would dress in his overalls, go to his small wood plant and treat wood from 4:30 a.m. until 8:30 a.m. He would then leave, take a quick shower, and dress for his law practice. "I had two black phones," Jimmy remembers. "The one on my left would ring and I'd answer, 'Jimmy Rane Law Office.' The one on my right would ring and I'd answer, 'Great Southern Wood Preserving,' and that's how I operated from 1971 until 1974. "In 1971, total sales for Great Southern Wood Preserving reached $22,000 – "not enough to cut the nut," Jimmy says. "We lost over $90,000 that year. And I'm looking like the village idiot. I had borrowed $76,000 from the bank, I am in debt $10,000 to the estate for equipment, and I'm on the hook for a ten-year land lease. By October of 1971, I'm nearly broke."

Law office of James W. Rane, 1971.

Jimmy knew he was in trouble, but he wasn't ready to bail out. "I walked into the bank and asked Mr. Noel Dowling, President of the Bank of Abbeville, for a $5,000 loan. I told him, 'Either I'll make it, or I'll close this business down. We'll hold an auction, sell everything, and whatever balance is left after the sale, I'll make monthly payments the rest of my life if that's what it takes to pay it off.

The original 1961 red International truck still sits in the Abbeville plant as a reminder of hard work and hard times.

After I listened to one of the worst beratings of my life for forty-five minutes, Mr. Dowling gave me the loan. I knew he would because I had brought the keys to my business with me. I had them in my hand and had he not given me the loan, they would have ended up on his desk."

Jimmy put that $5,000 into his bank account and the wheels started rolling. "I hopped in my 1961 red International truck (Jimmy still has it) and went to Marvin Tillis' lumber yard. I bought two bundles of 2x6x12's. Lawson Curry and I unloaded it, treated it, put it back on the truck and drove it to Ozark, Alabama. We sold those two bundles to Mr. Henry King at Ozark Building Supply for cash, brought that money back and put it in the bank. Later, we went back to Mr. Tillis and bought two more bundles. We did this over and over and over until I could buy one whole tractor-trailer load of lumber. You know the saying 'save a penny and it doubles every day?' That's how we came out of the crisis. And Ozark Building Supply is still a customer of ours to this day."

Brother Greg came on board in 1974. "He had a desk right beside mine. I put in an extension to one of the black telephones so he could listen to the conversations about wood. That's how he learned the business. Neither one of us knew a thing about wood when we started, but at least I had a head start on him."

In 1975, with the company still facing an uncertain future, an order came from a man who was buying treated lumber and exporting it to the Caribbean. The customer's first order was for $150,000 worth of wood, the largest ever received by the young company. Jimmy delivered the order and was promptly paid. Ecstatic, he thought he'd hit the mother lode. He would later discover just how wrong he was.

The orders from the man continued to come, and although he didn't pay as quickly, he paid according to the terms. That would soon change. After the biggest order of all, he paid only a portion of what was owed to Great Southern Wood. Jimmy pleaded with him to pay the rest, finally getting the debt down to $62,000. And for nine months, that's where it stayed.

One morning Mr. Tony walked into an astonished Jimmy's office, asking him if he had gotten his money. "I couldn't believe it," says Jimmy. "We never sat down and talked business, but he was vaguely aware of my problem with this customer."

"We need to go see him," said Mr. Tony.

"Yeah, we probably do," Jimmy responded.

"No, we need to go see him now. Make the reservations," Mr. Tony said.

Within two days, Jimmy and Mr. Tony paid the elusive customer a visit in Tortola, British Virgin Islands. It no longer mattered that Mr. Tony had not agreed with the decision to start the business. This was about family, and no one takes advantage of Mr. Tony's loved ones.

The pair flew from Atlanta to San Juan, Puerto Rico, via Eastern Airlines. From there, they flew "on a mosquito" to Roadtown, Tortola. They landed on a dirt strip and climbed into a light green 1957 Chevrolet Bel Aire taxi, instructing the driver to take them to the Treasure Island Hotel. The hotel looked like a set straight out of the Humphrey Bogart movie *Key Largo*. There was no air conditioning and no television in the rooms, only a radio. The bar was open air, and the meals were served family-style.

The next morning, they went to see their customer at his place of business. He owned a building supply store, repaired used Mercedes and resold them on the United States market, and owned a hotel. Jimmy was greeted warmly, but when he explained that the outstanding debt was crippling his business, the customer claimed he was unable to pay. For forty minutes, Mr. Tony stood quietly by, taking it all in, but not saying a word. Finally, he told Jimmy to let him speak to the reluctant customer alone.

Five minutes later, as Jimmy waited in the lumber yard, Mr. Tony and the store owner walked out of the office. The customer's face was ashen. He led the Ranes to his car; the three men drove to Barclays Bank, and the customer ordered a cashier's check for the full amount owed, plus interest. Mr. Tony smiles at the memory. Jimmy says, "To this day, I don't know what he said to the man."

Mr. Tony doesn't have to carry a big stick. His unbending demand for honesty and integrity speaks volumes to those who dare not live up to this simple truth. In his quiet way, Mr. Tony took Jimmy's bad customer to school and taught him lessons rooted in the deep, rich traditions of early Greenbush, lessons Mr. Tony himself learned as a boy while attending the School of Hard Knocks.

Great Southern Wood took off. "Jimmy started this thing. He promoted it to where it is today. He brought his brother Greg into the business as a partner in 1974," says Tony. It's a true family affair.

By 1976, Great Southern Wood had jumped from a meager $22,000 in sales to almost $1.4 million. The Rane brothers built a second plant in Mobile in hopes of becoming more competitive in that region. "Freight is a major part of our business, and a major expense," says Jimmy. "When we built the second plant, we eliminated a huge expense in freight charges. We thought it'd be a piece of cake, opening at that location, but it was a nightmare. Greg was at the new plant night and day for weeks, months at a time. Our execution wasn't great, but our strategy was wonderful. We were selling our product and making progress, but we were undercapitalized."

The business was almost growing out from under Jimmy and Greg. "The business was really strapped for cash," Jimmy recalls. "We were robbing Peter to pay Paul. It was amazing. I'd have to wait for people to pay an invoice before I could put money in the bank to pay our operating expenses. And we did this for years.

"The company was growing at thirty-something percent a year and was eating cash. The growth monkey eats two things: cash and people. So, I got this letter from the Harvard Business School in 1983, inviting me to apply for a business course. I knew we needed help, so I applied. It was the best thing I ever did."

The Harvard course is designed as an intense three-week stint of classes with no breaks and only one visit from friends or family. Three sessions are given over the course of three years, and all must be completed in order to graduate.

"Daddy and Mother drove me to Atlanta to catch the plane to Boston," Jimmy recalls. "When I left Great Southern, I left a stack of checks on my desk – I'm gone for three weeks, and it's hard to even call home. I'm in class six days a week, Monday through Saturday. I leave this pile of checks, $336,000 worth already written out. I tell my secretary, go to the post office every morning, open the mail, separate the checks, total up the amount of money you receive, and release that much in checks. That's how I was operating."

Mr. Tony sits on the edge of his chair as he listens to his son.

"Right before Jimmy goes to Harvard," Mr. Tony interjects, "my friend at the bank dies. His son takes over, and he's much more strict. I told him, 'You're hurting our business. Please stop sending the checks back. We've got the business. It's not that. It's just waiting in between.'"

Mr. Tony signed another note for $75,000; when the checks came in and Great Southern Wood's money was in temporary short supply, Mr. Tony's money covered. Mr. Tony might not have yet believed fully in his son's business, but he certainly believed in his son.

"I go to Harvard," Jimmy continues, "Within my first week, I knew what was wrong. We took five classes up there – marketing, control, finance, human aspects of business, and strategy. We studied by the case method system. In my finance class, the case we studied was Browning Lumber Company, can you believe it? On Thursday night, I'm crunching numbers and it's like you flipped on the light switch. I knew what was wrong with our business.

"Here I sit with a BA in business administration from Auburn, a law degree, and all these years of experience, and still I didn't really understand what was wrong with my company. It was terribly undercapitalized! So I go back home, call a friend of mine in Birmingham, and made an appointment with a bank. I made a presentation, and they give me a credit line instantly of one million dollars! The business zooms."

Jimmy's face still registers amazement when telling this story, although it's been over twenty years since the light came on for him. "I tell you, there were some dark days during the 1980s," says

Jimmy. "My marriage ended, and I was living above my law office with my son, and my daughter lived with her mother. I put one hundred percent of my effort into the business. That period of time was so intense, but I was so motivated because of what I had been through. There was really only one avenue left for me, and that was for me to succeed.

"That core strength," Jimmy says with conviction, "comes from Mr. Tony Rane. I have never been so motivated."

CHAPTER 21

Abbeville, Alabama

"La carità comincia a casa propria."

— *Charity begins at home.*

Jimmy and Greg pose for a photo just before their dive from the 10 foot board.

"We used to go to the beach a lot when the boys were growing up," Mr. Tony says. "You ought to see it down there now. All this new building, and people are buying up these condos and selling them before they ever move in for a hell of a profit. And they're not even on the water! The place we used to go, Palmetto Court, is being torn down and a seven-story hotel is being built in its place. They call it progress. Ha. There are nine townhouses beside the new hotel, all joined together, and we're number seven, just three doors down from the construction. There used to be time forever to enjoy that beach, but now there's not."

Seldom was the Rane family closer than on eagerly anticipated trips to Panama City for vacation. As the early morning sun glistened over the Gulf of Mexico, Mr. Tony and his sons would walk on the beach and catch crabs. They'd go swimming, then return, laughing, to their cabin. The tantalizing aromas of bacon cooking in the skillet and fresh, percolating coffee greeted them. Nights were for playing board games, barbecuing on a hot, small grill and talking in the intimate way only families enjoy. Spending time with his family is still what Mr. Tony enjoys doing most.

It was years later, on a family trip to the coast, when Mr. Tony stepped in at a crucial time and helped save Great Southern Wood. In the early years of the business, Jimmy and Greg would frequently disagree. The arguments got loud as the brothers tried to shout one another down. During this particular trip, Mr. Tony decided it was time for some fatherly advice. There can't be two bosses, he told his sons. "Every time we get together," he said, "it's nothing but fussing and fighting. If it's going to be like this," Mr. Tony continued, "I'd just as soon walk out this door, walk out in the Gulf, and just keep walking until I drown. That's what it's doing to me. One of you," he said, "has to step back."

His sons listened and responded. "Not only were we headed down the path of ruining our family relationship," Greg says, "but we were about to ruin our business." Eventually, Greg would give way to Jimmy, who started the business. The boys made room for each other by acknowledging their individual strengths, and the business grew and thrived. A crisis had been diffused by Mr. Tony's wisdom and by his love for his family.

In the infancy stages of Great Southern Wood, Jimmy needed help financing their growth. Mr.

Tony went to the bank and signed the note, placing him in an ownership position. He eventually divested himself completely of all Great Southern Wood stock before the company ran up in value, making Jimmy and Greg Rane the sole owners. "When things got to be pretty good and big," Mr. Tony says, "I decided to take my third and divide it between the two of them before Uncle Sam could come in and take most of it. Really the only way I helped them was to provide money when they had no collateral. The rest has been totally up to them."

It's obvious that Mr. Tony has provided more than money in hard times to Great Southern Wood. His emotional support is valued above all else, and when Jimmy and Greg speak with pride about their business, Mr. Tony beams with pride for his sons. One of Mr. Tony's favorite topics is the brilliant advertising campaign run by Great Southern, and Jimmy tells the story best.

"Capitalization of the company wasn't the only problem we had. We were locked into a situation where price was the only consideration in the purchase of our product. When I or any representative walked into a customer's business and said, 'Hi, we want to talk to you about treated lumber,' the first thing they'd say was, 'What's your price?' Well, we've got a great price, but let me tell you about our product. It's the finest treated wood, the highest quality. 'I don't care about any of that. What's your price, what's your price, what's your price?' It was so difficult.

"When I got to Harvard, one of the things we studied in marketing was commodity goods and how other companies had dealt with that. One of the other companies was Frank Perdue Chicken. A chicken's a chicken's a chicken, right? Well, Perdue was about to go bankrupt in 1968-1969, and just before going under, he decided to try something different. He started a marketing campaign that talked about his chickens being grain fed and kept off the ground, and he targeted this message to mothers who were very particular about what they were feeding their families. The rest is history. He turned his company around, made it into one of the largest in the country, and he did it through marketing.

Greg and Jimmy at the Conyers, Georgia plant, 1984.

"I got to thinking, how does that apply to my business? How can I replicate that? I wanted to find the most common thread that connects Alabama, Georgia, Tennessee, Florida, Mississippi, all the states I was selling my product in during the 1980s. What's the common trait? And what I came up with was college athletics. Everybody was passionate about their college team. How do I tap into that emotion, that passion, and ride along with it?"

Jimmy and Pat Dye on set of a TV shoot, with young James Jr.

Jimmy came home and called a good friend of his who had some connections in this arena. Years earlier, Pat Dye came to Abbeville and recruited a young man that Jimmy had coached in junior high school. Pat was an assistant coach at Alabama at the time, working as an assistant to Bear Bryant. Jimmy helped Pat connect with the very talented Leroy Cook, who went on to become a great All American for Alabama. Through this experience, Jimmy and Pat found common ground and became fast friends. It didn't hurt any that Jimmy was an Auburn alumnus and a supporter of their football program, of which Pat Dye was now the head coach.

"When I had this idea, I sat down and talked with Pat about it and asked him if he would be willing to help me and he said, 'yeah, sure.' So, we started out solely on his show with him endorsing

Great Southern. And it worked really well! It gave us a higher profile than we ever had, and we began to replicate it in other markets. We moved into all those other states, just rolled right along because it was working. Pat was instrumental in calling coaches and making contact for me, saying, 'Hey, I got this guy you really need to talk to'... he paved the way and made the introductions. Wimp Sanderson was a really good friend, too. We actually signed the basketball program at Alabama before we signed the football program. Wimp was instrumental in signing up Gene Stallings. Gene and I had great chemistry, still do. Because of my long-term relationship with both Pat and Gene, they both wound up on the Great Southern Board of Directors, and Wimp is on the board of the Jimmy Rane Foundation, our charitable organization."

This advertising works because the ads themselves are funny, the people are recognizable, and the emotional vein has been tapped. "There's humor in those ads," Mr. Tony says. "Plus, they aren't actors. They are actually people in the business doing this. The advertising strategy was altogether different from most, because it was funny. People remember Great Southern Wood ads because it's almost as if we're not selling anything. If you connect with a person, they will pay attention to the message."

"The first commercials were shot with actors, but they were flops," Jimmy says. "So, I

Jimmy and then Alabama coach, Gene Stallings.

Jimmy in TV spot with Coach Cliff Ellis.

Jimmy, with former Alabama basketball coach Wimp Sanderson, on set of their TV shoot.

Mr. Tony believed from the time his sons were born that athletics would help mold their character. He encouraged them to play sports and offered his unending support. Greg was a standout football player at Abbeville High School and Jimmy at Marion Military Institute. Mr. Tony rarely, if ever, missed a game.

called my old marketing professor in Boston, Marty Marshall, and talked to him about it. Marty said, 'Well, the reason Dave Thomas is in the Wendy's commercials is because they did research, and the public didn't believe the actors. But when Dave Thomas participated, the public thought, well, heck, he owns the company, he has credibility. That might be part of your problem.' OK, fine, I thought, we'll try that angle. And that's when I got in the commercials and I would have a line or two, but I didn't take myself seriously. I knew I wasn't an actor and that I was making a fool of myself, so I'd be the first one to laugh.

"It must work, though, because yesterday at a meeting, I went into the restaurant to get some breakfast and was seated beside Norman Lumpkin. He's a former news broadcaster, highly respected and well thought of, and he looks and me and said, 'You're Jimmy Rane!' and I said, 'You're Norman Lumpkin!' and we both laughed, shook hands, and exchanged pleasantries. Norman said, 'You must have a sense of humor as big as you are, because your commercials are so funny.'"

Jimmy's face is recognizable, even in Tucson, Arizona. While pumping gas, Jimmy was greeted by a customer who walked out of the convenience store and recognized the YellaWood Man. In the business of marketing, it's difficult to give a product a personality, and Jimmy has done that. "When you look at the research, we have brand name product identification that most companies would pay millions of dollars for," Jimmy says. "I mean, it's huge. The brand name recognition we have is particularly high in places like Atlanta, New Orleans, Orlando, Tampa, Nashville, huge metro markets. To have that kind of equity is a great accomplishment."

"I think people want to be a part of your company because of those commercials," says Mr. Tony. And he is right. There is something about momentum that gets everyone going, and Great Southern Wood continues to go in a positive direction. "When people say, 'Hey, I saw your commercials during the game yesterday,' it makes the people who work for us feel good," says Jimmy. "Our employees feel a sense of ownership and pride. And we're busy! Great Southern does its best work when the plate is full."

...

From the days when he and other boys in Greenbush walked up the street to a neighborhood park to play baseball and football, sports have been part of Tony Rane's life. He was no great athlete, but he thrived on honest and fierce competition. It is a trait that helped him become an immensely successful businessman in his adult years.

Young Tony wanted badly to play football at Central High School in Madison, but he was never quite talented enough. He loved baseball, but there was no real opportunity to play on an organ-

"When I was coming up and playing ball at Abbeville High School, Dad was heavily involved in the Holiday Inns," remembers Greg. "He never missed a single ballgame I played, not one." On one weekend that is fresh in Greg's mind to this day, Mr. Tony was going through a Holiday Inn training session in Memphis. He left Memphis on Friday, drove almost 500 miles to Abbeville, and arrived in time to watch the game. When the game ended, Mr. Tony drove right back to Memphis.

ized level. He even tried his hand at boxing. Boxing, he thought, might just be his sport.

"The university had a boxing team, and there were two guys from our neighborhood that were undefeated in college competition," Mr. Tony says. "We had boxing teams in high school, too. I tried out and had some success, but I got the you-know-what beat out of me some, too." Little could young Tony have known in those years that he would one day count among his friends some well known names in college athletics. He certainly couldn't have known that the plush reception area at the Auburn University Football Complex would be called the "Anthony J. Rane Reception Center."

When Great Southern Wood began sponsoring college football coaches' television shows, Jimmy introduced his father to some of the nation's great coaches, and solid friendships were born. Men who are tremendously successful in their own right listen to Mr. Tony with a mixture of respect, awe and fascination. "Mr. Tony is something else," Gene Stallings says. "I think the best thing I could say about him is the best thing you can say about anybody – he is a man of his word. If he tells you something, you can believe it. If he says he's going to do something, he's going to do it, no matter what it costs him. He has a great sense of humor and tells some great stories. At his age, he has more energy than most of us have."

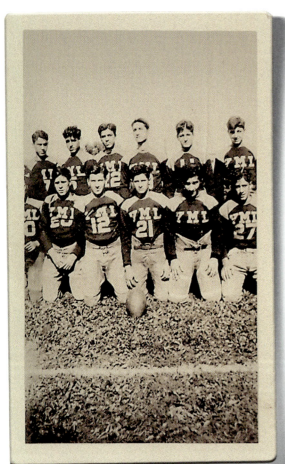

Mr. Tony's high school football team. Mr. Tony is on the back row, second from right.

"I've sat down and talked about his past and how he's handled his business, how he's seen things change in this country for good and bad," says Tommy Tuberville, Auburn football coach. "He's a real common sense kind of guy. He understands people. I think the reason he's been successful is because he's able to deal with different types of people in different parts of the country."

The "Anthony J. Rane Reception Center" in the Auburn University Football Complex.

When Tuberville recruits players for his team, his travels may take him to a poverty-stricken family or to the home of a corporate executive officer. "Mr. Tony would have no problem relating to either family," says Tuberville. "He probably could have been a great coach. He definitely could have been a great recruiter. See, Mr. Tony doesn't force his advice on anyone. But he's ready to offer help in matters of business and life in general if he's asked.

"He's low key and keeps his opinion to himself unless he's asked for it. He's a great listener," continues Tuberville. "When you ask for his opinion, he'll give it and back it up with substantial experience. We'll talk about politics, sports, almost anything. And his opinions are right on target."

Pat Dye, a tough, hard-nosed man with little patience for those who lack fortitude, found a kindred soul in Mr. Tony. "Anytime there is greatness achieved, there is always a strong foundation. That's where Mr. Tony enters his boys' lives. He's all about the backbone, the guts, the character and the fundamentals you live by. That's what I see when I see him, a guy who instilled in his sons the value of a work ethic and the strong character it takes to be successful with your family and in the business world."

Now Mr. Tony's name is forever linked to the game he loves. He was shocked the day he learned that the reception room at the Auburn Football Complex would bear his name. And it's not just an ordinary reception room – it's the room that houses Heisman Trophies won by Pat Sullivan and Bo Jackson, as well as other valuable pieces of Auburn's history. "That was quite unexpected and a tremendous thing," Mr. Tony says. "I can't tell you how much that meant to me."

(Seated L-R) Coach Larry Blakeney, Coach Tommy Tuberville, A.J. "Tony Rane" (Standing L-R) Greg Rane, Coach Pat Dye, Attorney Don Lusk, CEO Jimmy Rane, The Honorable Senator Lowell Barron, Coach Wimp Sanderson, Frank Robertson

June 24, 2000 to June 30, 2000

For Larry Blakeney, Troy University football coach, Mr. Tony's life is about more than just interesting stories. It's about life lessons.

"I've probably known Mr. Tony for 20 years or more but it wasn't until we went on a trip to Canada that I really got to know him. One leg of our trip took place by train and I sat next to Mr. Tony for hours totally engrossed in listening to him tell parts of his life story. It took about two days for me to get the whole story out of him and I was completely spellbound by it. I remember saying to him – 'You should write a book about your life!' There are just so many "life lessons" that we can all learn from Mr. Tony."

For many years, Mr. Tony's athletic exploits were limited to the golf course and attending Auburn games. Before being sidelined with macular degeneration, he played golf frequently with a group of friends knows as "The Hackers." The Hackers claim 39 members with an average age of around 75. Three members are in their 90s. Dusty Rhodes, a long-time member of the Hackers, laughs as he describes Mr. Tony's golf game. "Tony's a good man," he says, "but he wasn't a good golfer. He could hit the ball a long way, but he didn't know where it was going."

Kenneth Lane, another Hacker, says the tee times were about fun, fellowship and jokes, always jokes. "We played for big money," Lane says. "We played for a dollar and a half. The way we are about that money, somebody might get killed over two dollars. See, Tony's last name used to be Lane, but some of his people robbed a bank and he changed it to Rane."

The Dothan Country Club may not claim the Hackers as among their youngest members, but it would be hard pressed to find a group with as much energy and camaraderie. "Tony has always told more jokes than anybody," Lane says. "Some of them are a little shady, but that doesn't stop us from laughing."

"While he can't join us on the course anymore, we still see each other at the club and I can tell you that all of us are enriched for having known Tony Rane."

CHAPTER 22

Abbeville, Alabama, USA, July, 2004

"Il sangue non è acqua."

— *Blood is thicker than water.*

The memories for Greg and Jimmy are long and sweet. Jimmy recalls when the family lived in a one-bedroom apartment, long before the days of vacations at the shore. Jimmy got a pup tent for his birthday that year and couldn't wait to camp out in the small yard outside the apartment. That night, Mr. Tony squeezed into the small tent with him. They told stories until it was time to go to sleep.

"I had a white duck for a pet when we lived there, and he lived in the yard," Jimmy remembers. "Daddy and I were sleeping in a tent made for a child, and Daddy slept with his head protruding from the tent because he was too big to fit inside. The moon was shining on Daddy's bald head, and maybe the duck thought it was an egg. Daddy woke up in the middle of the night with that duck pecking on his head. That ended the first camping trip. We went back inside."

Not only ducks were drawn by Mr. Tony's animal magnetism. Even the neighborhood dogs benefited from his generosity. "When Tony would come home from the Holiday Inn," says Ms. Libba, "the dogs all knew the sound of his car and would meet him in the driveway because Tony always had a sack of bones for them." Mr. Tony has a fondness for all animals, but will not share his home with another because "when you lose them, well, it's devastating," he says. "We've had three dogs in our lifetime. A Collie and two German Shepherds. Libba would like another, but..."

Jimmy's persona changes from man to boy as he remembers his favorite childhood dog, Flip, a white Collie that was also special to Mr. Tony. "I'm not sure how old I was when this happened, but I was really young, maybe four or five," Jimmy says. "There was a ladder propped up against the back of the hotel (Frances Hotel) that led to the roof, probably because of some repairs. Being a boy, I had to go

From the time Jimmy was born in 1946 and Greg in 1952, they came first in the lives of Tony and Libba Rane. "He was a very strict dad, but he was a very caring dad," Ms. Libba says. "The children knew he was strict, but they also knew he loved them."

Jimmy Rane and Flip, the family's favorite dog.

up that ladder. I was almost to the top when I heard Flip barking. I looked down and he was at the bottom of the ladder, like he was trying to get me to come down.

"He ran around to the back door of the restaurant barking his head off until he got Daddy's attention. When Flip came back, Daddy was right behind him. Flip stood up and put his front paws as far up as he could reach on the rungs of that ladder, and looked up and barked to show Daddy what I was doing. I wasn't sure if I liked that or not at the time, because I got in trouble, but later I realized that Flip probably saved me from serious injury or worse."

"I loved that dog like a child," Mr. Tony sadly says. "He got hit by a car. I hate it. But, before that, he would come in the house and sit right by my side. You just get to love those dogs. I'm glad to have the memories, but don't want to go through it again."

• • •

In the early days after the war, especially for veterans, a

party, care-free atmosphere was palpable. Young families began to put down roots. Life was relatively free from worry; there were no limits to what might be accomplished through hard work and sheer determination. During this exciting time, Mr. Tony and Ms. Libba turned their home into a favorite destination for friends seeking good food, music and fun in the company of their most intimate companions. The couple's unmatched ability to turn any occasion into a special event was legendary. Every week, sometimes two or three nights per week, a group of people would gather at the Rane home for dinner or drinks – a casual picnic on the patio or a formal, dress-up soiree – and this open graciousness was part of the seamless connection that Mr. Tony and Ms. Libba shared.

Kids were all smiles at Jimmy's sixth birthday party themed after Alice In Wonderland.

"I remember a party one night right after we moved in our house," Jimmy recalls. "It was in 1953, and the house was practically empty of furniture. Mother and Daddy set up two card tables – one with food and one with drinks – plugged in the radio, and had a dance party. It was the perfect place for it because there wasn't much furniture. Gosh, the sound of all those feet dancing on the hardwood floors ... I can still hear it!"

Ms. Libba's natural flair for décor was shared with her children, too. Jimmy recalls his 6th birthday party, when all the guests dressed up

Roadside picnics while on the family vacations.

like characters from Alice In Wonderland. "Everything seemed just like 'Wonderland' – particularly to a bunch of six-year-olds. Mother could really throw a party," he says. "There was such detail and extravagance. The time it took to make the costumes alone ... it's amazing to remember that far back," he laughs.

For Jimmy and Greg, family vacations were among the best parties of all. Mr. Tony would take a week or two off in the summer and the family would visit the Great Smoky Mountains, Chicago, Niagara Falls, and other beautiful destinations. But, the journey to reach the destination is where the fun began. "We'd always stay in hotels and eat in restaurants when we got to our final point," Jimmy remembers, "but we rarely ate in restaurants along the way. Instead, Daddy would pack a Coleman stove and thermos, and he would cook for us at roadside picnic tables. That was sometimes my favorite part of the trip! Everything we did was special because he and Mother made it that way."

• • •

Maureen Floyd and Libba Mills were childhood friends, the closest of friends, and grew up together in Abbeville. Charles C. Vickrey was a farm security agent for Henry County and roomed at the Frances Hotel. When the hotel was filled, Ms. Murphy, the owner, would arrange for Tony to stay in Vickrey's room and sleep in his extra bed.

"Through my wife-to-be, Libba, and Vickrey's girlfriend and future wife, Maureen, we became friends," says Mr. Tony of he and Charles. "Later, Vickrey entered the service to go into the Air Cadets. Now, here I am from Wisconsin and they send me to Camp Rucker in Alabama. Vickrey's from Abbeville and they send him to Truex Field in Madison. I told my family, and they met him and fed him dinner while he was a cadet. The core of it is that we courted our girlfriends together, and partied together, and danced together. We were pals forever."

After the war, both couples settled in Abbeville; Tony and Charles established businesses and built houses across the street from one another. "Vickrey had the opportunity to buy about twelve or so acres where our home is now," recalls Mr. Tony. "He was the first one to build out here – that's why our road is named Vickrey Drive. As a result, being as close friends as we were, what better place for us to build a house than with people who we've known the whole time I've been in the South? We bought our land from Vickrey and built our house in 1953."

The subdivision was designed and built in a very modern way, ahead of the times for a small town. In the city of Abbeville, there had never been a development like it, with an exclusive one-way

Time with friends came often and was treasured.

entrance off of a main road, with the houses set back on the large lots, and all of the homes of similar size and character. It was the first restricted neighborhood in Abbeville. Only five families lived in the small locality, and the Ranes were the third to build.

The Vickreys had three girls, and the Ranes had two boys. The children grew up playing together. The two couples traveled the world together and spent most of their leisure hours joined in social activity.

The Vickrey's oldest daughter, Catherine, married one of Jimmy Rane's very best friends, Lester Killabrew. Now, Lester and Catherine are Jimmy's neighbors, and their children have grown up with Jimmy's children. When Maureen Vickrey died, Jimmy Rane delivered the eulogy at her funeral. The families continue to be close to this day. "Maureen and Charles Vickrey, and Daddy and Mother, added a new sense of style and grace to the town,' Jimmy says proudly.

Maureen and Charles with Mr. Tony and Miss Libba in Venice, Italy, 1977.

• • •

In a Birmingham hotel in 1972, Mr. Tony put his life at risk to protect his wife. The Ranes had cheered Auburn's 17-16 victory over Alabama earlier in the day and had gone out with friends that night. They were back in their hotel room getting ready for bed. Libba had put on her nightgown and Tony was in the bathroom when a knock came on the door. Mr. Libba opened the door as Mr. Tony came up behind her. A strange man said he was coming in. Mr. Tony moved his wife out of the way, put his hand up in front of the man, and said, "No, hell, you're not!" The man put a gun to Mr. Tony's stomach and walked in.

A few months prior to that night, a friend of Mr. Tony's experienced the nightmare of someone breaking and entering into his home, tying him up, and raping his wife. The incident was fresh on Mr. Tony's mind as the agitated man entered the room. He told them he was going to stay for thirty minutes and no one would be hurt. "I told the man to leave, that if he left, I wouldn't call the police," remembers Mr. Tony, "but he wouldn't leave. He refused." The man glared at Mr. Tony, his eyes flashing, and said, "Do you want to die?" Mr. Tony quickly responded, "Hell no! Do you want to go to the electric chair?"

Mr. Tony's heart was pounding, but he stayed calm, looking the dangerous intruder in the eye. "I thought if I acted scared it would make things worse," says Mr. Tony. "I finally convinced him to let me put my clothes on and we would go downstairs and leave like we were friends." The man agreed. They rode the elevator down and it stopped. Charles Chapman, a friend of Mr. Tony's from Dothan, Alabama, and his daughter got on. Charles was unaware of the danger the man with Mr. Tony presented, but his daughter later questioned him to her father, stating, "Who was that man with Mr. Tony?" A child's instinct is often right on. The elevator stopped again and Charles and his daughter got off. The elevator continued down to the lobby floor. The man wanted Mr. Tony to go out the back

Catherine and Jimmy, ages four and five.

door to the parking lot. Mr. Tony said, "OK." But as soon as the man took a step toward the back door, Mr. Tony bolted to the lobby desk instead and enlisted help. The police were summoned, but the man was nowhere to be found. There was news the next morning that a man had forced his way into a room at a nearby hotel and shot someone. "It was scary," says Mr. Tony. "I wasn't all that brave, but if I'd showed I was the least bit afraid, there's no telling what he would have done. I had to do all I could to protect my wife."

Mr. Tony clearly understands there are times you simply have to stand up for yourself and Birmingham was one of those times. It's the same life-long lesson he taught Jimmy at the young age of eight.

Like most children his age, Jimmy would spend hours playing outside when he came home from school each day. When he was seven or eight, Libba noticed that he seemed to change. When she asked him, "Why don't you go outside and play?" – the truth came out.

There was a bully at school who was picking on Jimmy and he didn't want to risk a confrontation with him.

When Mr. Tony found out about it, instead of being sympathetic, he turned to Jimmy and said, "What are you going to do about it?" I told Daddy I was scared and that I didn't want to do anything about it.

Daddy's eyes narrowed and he looked at me in a stern way. "You're going to stand up to him or you'll get a whipping from me. When you go to school tomorrow, don't fight him there. Tell him you'll meet him after school or off of school property."

I don't think I've ever been as frightened as I was standing there in front of my Dad at that moment. Faced with the prospect of being whipped by the bully or being whipped by my Daddy, the choice was easy.

The next day I went to school and the fight was set for Saturday morning at the library in uptown Abbeville at 10 o'clock.

When Daddy came home that night, he asked me what had happened and I told him. He said, "OK, you come to my furniture store before you go to the library Saturday morning."

Jimmy, first grade, 1952.

I think that walk from our little apartment to Daddy's furniture store was the longest walk of my life. All I could think about was how frightened I was.

When I got to Daddy's store, no one was there but Daddy and me. He sat down next to me and looked me dead in the eyes and said, "Jimmy, you've got to stand up for yourself. If you don't, you'll be running for the rest of your life."

He then reached in his pocket and pulled out a small role of Lifesavers. He took my right hand

and opened it and placed the roll of Lifesavers between my fingers. Then, he rolled my fingers into a fist and held it tight. He looked me in the eyes again and said, "Jimmy, you hold these in your hand real tight and you walk right up to him, don't say hello, nice to see you, or anything. Just look him in the eyes, keep walking and hit him as hard as you can, right in the mouth. Then, no matter what, keep right on hitting him!"

You know, I can't tell you what it was about those Lifesavers but they sure gave me some confidence.

So, I walked from the furniture store up to the Courthouse, across the lawn to the library and there he was. He was standing there with a couple of his buddies and when he saw me he started mocking me, saying, "Here comes that old chicken!"

Just as Daddy instructed, I never said a word, just kept walking. And he started walking toward me. I guess he thought I was going to run like I had always done. But when he got close enough, I hit him as hard as I could right in the mouth. It stunned him and he went down flat on his back.

I didn't stop with one punch. He started crying, "Don't hit me anymore."

To tell you the truth, it stunned me, too. I told him to never mess with me again then I turned and walked away.

"Through good times and bad times, it was a good life," says Miss Libba. We had time together, and we made time together as a family. Anything the children were in – plays, ballgames – Tony was there. I'd live it all over again any day." Tony echoes his wife's sentiment: "We had a good routine. We just managed it and things fell in line. Libba and I were partners. It didn't seem that we were beating our brains out at all. We were teaching our children the importance of honesty and character, of finding creative and fun ways to do things together, and how important it is not let people take advantage of you or push you around."

• • •

Mr. Tony believed from the time his sons were born that athletics would help mold their character. He encouraged them to play sports and offered his unending support. Greg was a standout football player, an Alabama All-State tackle at Abbeville High School, and Jimmy excelled on the field at Marion Military Institute. Mr. Tony rarely, if ever, missed a game.

"When I was coming up and playing ball at Abbeville High School, Dad was heavily involved in the Holiday Inns," remembers Greg. "He never missed a single ballgame I played, not one." On one weekend that is fresh in Greg's mind to this day, Mr. Tony was going through a Holiday Inn training session in Memphis. He left Memphis on Friday, drove almost 500 miles to Abbeville, and arrived in

"He will always be my dad, but now, from a man-to-man point of view, I view him probably as my best friend," says Greg. *"I have a lot of friends, but he's my best friend, my best confidant. I feel very, very fortunate."*

time to watch the game. When the game ended, Mr. Tony drove right back to Memphis.

Though his business ventures consumed great chunks of Mr. Tony's time, he and Ms. Libba always found time for their sons, even when it was least expected. Jimmy went sadly with his Marion Military Academy teammates for a football game at Sewanee Military Academy. His parents told him it was too far, that they weren't coming. But Mr. Tony found a way. "I just couldn't believe that I was going to play and he wasn't going to be there," Jimmy recalls. "When we came out on that field and he was standing there, that's the most inspired game I ever played in my life."

Not all of the memories were sweet at the time, however. One night, at the age of 15, Jimmy went with friends to a basketball game in Headland. He and two friends were dropped off at the Rane house after the game, where they played records and gulped soft drinks. As the hour grew late, Jimmy's friends wondered how they were getting home. Instead of waking up his sleeping parents, Jimmy, who had a learner's permit, took his friends home in his father's truck. As he pulled back into the driveway, he got the feeling only a teenager caught in an act of defiance can get. The lights were on in the kitchen. When he walked through the door, Mr. Tony stood there in his pajamas, belt in hand. "Why did you take my truck?" Mr. Tony asked. Jimmy explained that his friends didn't have a ride home, but the explanation wasn't going well.

"Haven't I told you that you're not allowed to drive by yourself? You took my truck and you don't have a license to drive!" Mr. Tony said. Jimmy felt the sting of the belt that night, and he can still feel it to this day. "My wife wanted to divorce me," Mr. Tony says, laughing now at the memory. "I really did whip him unmercifully. I was scared to death, and when I saw that he was all right, that fear turned to anger. I never again had to whip him."

In Mr. Tony's value system, there is also a time to admit you are wrong, even to your children. When Greg and Jimmy were teens, Greg bent the front wheel on Mr. Tony's car one night, and Mr. Tony scolded Jimmy severely for a crime he didn't commit. "I later found out it was Greg who had hit a curb and done the damage," Mr. Tony says. "When I found out, I sat up and waited for Jimmy to come home so I could apologize to him," Mr. Tony remembers, "because I had been unmerciful with him. I told him, 'Son, don't let anybody, not even me, talk to you like I did the other day.'" Those are the precious moments that are critical turning points in a child's relationship with a parent, and Mr. Tony rose to the occasion. Love is stronger than pride.

Mr. Tony's two sons remember the tender moments when they knew beyond any doubt they were loved without condition. It's the little things, special and unique, that have given Mr. Tony complete access to the keys that open his boys' hearts. Love is the reward.

Says Jimmy of his father: "He is the essential, strong pillar for me. His approval and his opinion matter more than anybody's. I don't think you can have that kind of influence without standing the test of time."

In an often confusing and frightening world, seven grandchildren found sanctuary and unconditional love at Mr. Tony and Ms. Libba's comfortable home. The Ranes were never too busy for Jimmy's three children and Greg's four. The door was always open. Most of the children are adults now, making their own way in the world, but they are still drawn back to the loving home on Vickrey Drive and the warmth of their grandparents' embrace.

"I don't know what the proper words are," says Mr. Tony, as he describes his relationship with his grandchildren. "They really make my life. You get to do things with your grandchildren that you couldn't do with your children. They are so special to us that it's hard for me to put into words. And now, the great-grandchildren are arriving!"

Through moves, divorces and the tribulations of youth, one constant in the lives of the grandchildren was their grandparents' home. They remember the aromas wafting from the kitchen, the warmth of snuggling into bed with Mr. Tony and Ms. Libba, the boxes of chocolates their grandfather always shared with them.

The circle of love grows ever larger, and Mr. Tony is its centerpoint. He remains a beacon of light, a safe port in a storm, for his extended family. Mr. Tony is the steadying force, the solid foundation, for all who love him. His circle will not be broken.

CHAPTER 23

Abbeville, Alabama

"Vivi e lascia vivere."

— *Live and let live.*

"Sometimes after Mass, we visit our son or our granddaughter," says Mr. Tony. "But sometimes, it's just the two of us, coming back home for a drink and dinner." Either option suits Mr. Tony just fine, and his face softens momentarily as he considers being home alone with his bride. He and Ms. Libba are still intrigued by each other after all these years; the energy they exchange is palpable. "She's my inspiration, no doubt," says Mr. Tony, a sentiment he often repeats in reference to Ms. Libba. "But the thing I like about her the most is, she is what she is. She doesn't put on the dog. What you see is what you get. I like that. Libba doesn't try to find fault with people. She's the shining example of integrity."

Ms. Libba has only a small reaction to Mr. Tony's latest passionate gush. "There's five years difference in our ages. He's my older man," she kids. "It's just right, that age difference. That's what I tell my granddaughters anyway… look up there in that parking lot, all that is Wal-Mart. It's a city. It's too much! I've only been there twice and that was two times too many." Parking lots bore Ms. Libba,

Wherever he went on his journey, Mr. Tony always found a church where he could worship.

perhaps because there aren't any passing lanes.

Saturday night Mass fulfills Mr. Tony's Sunday obligation. "It's called Vigil Mass," says Mr. Tony. "The mass we're saying tonight is the same all over the world. So, if I'm in Helsinki, I'm listening to the same mass they're listening to in Dothan. Isn't that wonderful?"

Mr. Tony is a man whose faith is deeply rooted, a man who thanks God every day for his many blessings and understands what it means to give and to receive. Faith sustained his parents when they were apart for five years after Giuseppe Reina left Sicily for the promise of a better life in America. It has sustained Mr. Tony through the trials and tribulations of life, and it sustains him still.

"Every morning and every night I pray to the Lord and thank Him for what he has done for me," Mr. Tony says. "That's not just idle chatter. I try to say the Rosary every day. It's just a habit of mine. When I was coming up, I wasn't all that good, but my faith was always strong. I believed in the forgiveness of Jesus Christ, and I still do."

Mr. Tony is the first and only Catholic in the small town of Abbeville, and in the early days he was pressured to change churches. "I was told that the best thing for my business was for me to join an Abbeville church. I explained to the man that I went to church every Sunday in Eufaula, and I told him that would not change. The man was well-meaning, but he didn't understand the depth of my loyalty to my Catholic upbringing.

"I'm going to church," Mr. Tony says. "It's not to satisfy the priest; it is to satisfy my spiritual inner feelings, to satisfy my need to be close to God." Mr. Tony's faith isn't just about showing up for Mass or contributing money. It's about the way one lives. He believes in treating people the way he would like to be treated and makes that a cornerstone of his life. He was a tough and aggressive businessman, but at the core of it all was his determination to be honest, to be fair, and to let the light of his faith shine through.

In the exciting days before they were married, Tony and Libba were warned that religion would be a problem in their marriage. Some people actually believed that it would be best if they reconsidered making a vow to each other, as Libba was a Baptist. After over 60 years of marriage, Mr. Tony laughs at that notion. "It's never been a problem, not even for one day. Our different religions have never interfered in our marriage. Sometimes I'll go to church with her, and sometimes she'll go with me."

Tony and Libba were married by a Baptist preacher, but in order to receive the sacrament of communion and for his marriage to be recognized by his church, Tony and Libba had to agree that their children would be raised as Catholics. Libba had no objection, and they were married again by a Catholic chaplain, sealing the deal on both sides.

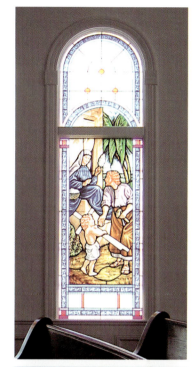

This stained glass window is dedicated in honor of Ms. Libba, First Baptist Church, Abbeville.

Jimmy was a Catholic until the age of nine. He went to a revival one evening with his mother and was moved by a fiery Baptist preacher. He switched teams fairly early on and, as an adult, became a Methodist. Greg remained a Catholic into his adult years before he became an Episcopalian. "I never had a problem with it," Ms. Libba says. "The children went to church with their dad when they were little. When they were old enough to choose, we let them choose. I told my preacher, 'I'm Baptist, but you won't believe my family. My husband is Catholic, Jimmy is Methodist and Greg is Episcopalian.' He just hollered! It doesn't matter. We're all going to the same place anyway."

"He always smelled so good," says Ms. Libba of Mr. Tony.

Mr. Tony says he never had a problem with his sons' decisions about the church. What is important, he says, is that his sons and grandchildren are strong in their faith. But, for him, Catholicism is part of the very fabric of Mr. Tony's soul. However, he contributes to both his and Ms. Libba's churches. "I believe commitment goes beyond a denomination, beyond loyalty to one church or another. I believe Christianity is about helping others, not about glitz and glitter," Mr. Tony says. "I think God intended for us to be good to one another, to serve Him, to love Him, and to be good to other people." That belief and commitment carry through every part of his life. Mr. Tony walks the walk.

Even as a young man, Tony Rane never questioned God, not even for a day. "That's one of the mysteries in the Bible," Mr. Tony says. "If you were to start questioning everything, life wouldn't be worth living. Think if we didn't have the Bible to go by, what kind of chaos we would have in our world. You have to satisfy your own inner feelings, not someone else's. I try to mind my business and to do what I think is right. I deal with what I can control. I can't control anybody else, not even my children.

"One of the great things is forgiveness. I try to forgive everybody. I don't forget, but I try to forgive them. If you forget, the same mistake could happen again. In spite of all the things that have come up lately, like priests making headline news for questionable actions, I don't go to church for them," Mr. Tony says. "I go to church to satisfy my spiritual life, not to hear the priest.

"I go to church to satisfy my soul."

**"I can get my family in a lot of trouble,"
Ms. Libba laughingly says.**

CHAPTER 24

Cammarata, Italy

"L'appetito vien mangiando."
— *Appetite comes with eating.*

Almost thirty years ago, Mr. Tony and Ms. Libba made their first trip to Italy. "We didn't know where we were going, and we were trying to find some of Tony's people," recalls Ms. Libba. "We went through this little town and there was a shepherd with all of his sheep in the middle of the road. It was so beautiful. We drove all over Italy, eating bread and drinking wine."

"It was 1976, and we flew into Milan, picked up a car, and drove into Sicily," Mr. Tony clarifies. "We stayed in this little hotel near Cammarata, and I told the guy who ran the place why I was there. Well, he had worked with the Allies during World War II and spoke English. We went to our room and about an hour later, the man called and said, 'I want to let you know that your cousin is coming to pick you up in about thirty minutes.' 'My cousin!' I said. I was a little bit leery.

"I told Libba that she'd have to stay at the hotel while I checked it out. She said, 'Not me, I'm going with you.' Sure enough, in thirty minutes this young man picked us up and took us to

Alfredo's famed restarant – Rome, Itlay.

Cammarata where his sister and her husband lived. At that time, I only had one uncle left, my mother's brother, Uncle Joe (Bongiovanni). I was still a little leery until the woman whose home we were in left for a moment and came back carrying a picture of my sister and mother that had been sent to them from the United States. Then I knew it was real. We only spent about three hours with them as we had to drive back to Rome and catch our flight to the States."

Mr. Tony corresponded with his Italian relatives throughout the years. And in 1995, almost twenty years after the first meeting with his uncle and cousins, Mr. Tony wrote again, this time to announce his planned stop in Cammarata with twelve members of his immediate family. The group, known affectionately as the Rane Thirteen, would arrive Cammarata by bus.

"We landed in Palermo," remembers Ms. Libba. "That's where the bus picked us up. We traveled to Argigento where we stayed at the Hotel Kaos about 30 minutes from Cammarata."

On the day of their visit to Cammarata, the Rane Thirteen piled into the bus and headed up the mountain. However, the village's roads weren't as wide as the bus. Cousins sent cars down the narrow mountain road to retrieve the family and safely deliver them to the home of Uncle Joe's daughter, Concetta, and her husband Biaggio Lupo.

Jimmy's daughter Ashleigh tells the tale: "We were a diverse group. Dad and Uncle Greg were on a mission to discover their roots, and there were a bunch of nineteen to twenty-one year old cousins ready to explore, and then a nine year old, plus wives, mothers and our grandmother. We were like the Griswalds," she laughs. "Here come all these Americans on a bus floating into Cammarata. And we're going to visit the family, but nobody there speaks English. Our bus driver, who already hated us for being spoiled Americans, was aggravated because the bus wouldn't fit in the streets; he chain smoked the entire time. We had to stop the bus and arrange transportation up that mountain. They sent one of those little European compacts and our cousin didn't speak English, when all of a sudden, Uncle Greg said, 'La famiglia!' That's all he knew how to say. It cracked us up.

"When we first got to the house, our relatives started serving us all homemade wine," says Ashleigh. "It was potent and knocking us off the charts. We were feeling pretty ripe after that. All the young kids could do was sit around and laugh and watch what happened next. See, Dee Dee (Mr. Tony) was the only one who could speak any Italian. At one point we're all sitting in the living room and Grandmother started talking in English, saying to them, 'Oh, who is that in the photograph, she's so lovely,' and they'd smile and gesture. Grandmother wanted so much to use her Southern belle charm on them, but they couldn't understand her. It just tickled us all."

"I could understand every word they were saying," reflects Mr Tony, "but I couldn't express

Nearly 100 years after Guiseppe Reina left Italy for America,

The Rane Thirteen enters the city Guiseppe left thus creating a living legacy.

'The Ranes' meet 'The Bongiovannis.' Although the language barrier was difficult, the love, comfort and hospitality of family overcame any communication gap.

myself very well. They would fill in the words for me, and the Italian came back. It had been sixty-some years since I had spoken it, or even heard it every day."

The well-respected European tradition of long lunches was a highlight of the Cammarata trip for the adults, but was lost on the children. "At first they brought out a pasta dish, and we thought it was over, but that was just the beginning," Ashleigh remembers. "Then the second course comes, then the third, and there's no end to it. The entire meal lasted at least two hours. It's a neat tradition, but just don't factor out that there are six spoiled-rotten college kids on this trip, and we didn't really appreciate what was going on at the time. We were all at the wrong age, too wild then, to get the most out of this trip. The good thing is, although we didn't appreciate every aspect of it, we all enjoyed being together as a family. Looking back on it, we were just a bunch of dumb kids craving McDonalds instead of five-star Italian cuisine. It was unfortunate that we weren't able to understand and appreciate the experience fully."

"Well, my plan was to take everybody out to lunch," says Mr. Tony. "But when we got there, they had cooked a feast for us. It was outstanding."

"It might have been a little much for the kids," agrees Jimmy. "But, from my perspective, we didn't have a bad meal the entire time we were there. The Italian culture is, after all, about food."

Jimmy lovingly remembers the trip to Cammarata. "We got to the house and there were my dad's first cousins and other relatives. We spent the day and ate and talked. After a while, it doesn't matter if you speak the same language. It's like any other family outing. If you were to go to any family reunion, you would arrive, everyone would look, and touch, and hug, then you'd immediately be given something to eat and drink."

Ashleigh interjects, "Reflecting back on the trip, I realize what an incredible opportunity we were all given. Most people are told about their lineage. We were able to experience it, and in many ways it was like going back in time because many of the traditions are the same. Much of the landscape is the same. We were literally walking in the same places and looking at the same images as our ancestors. How many people are given such a wonderful link to their past?"

Mr. Tony sums the trip up succinctly. "It was exquisite," he says.

Photographs show the American Rane Thirteen wrapped arm in arm with their Italian family, holding hands as if it's the most natural thing in the world to allow love to bridge their communication gaps. And it is. One need not be Italian to appreciate this truth, only to have a heart willing to travel the distance.

CHAPTER 25

Home

"A tavola con i buoni amici e famiglia non s'invecchia."

– *At the table with good friends and family you do not become old.*

Mr. Tony has known poverty. He has known discrimination because of his Italian heritage. But his beliefs never wavered. Patience is a virtue, Mr. Tony acknowledges, but he has little patience for those who turn their backs on his country and its ideals of freedom and compassion, or for those who want to sample the fruits of freedom without accepting the responsibility that goes with it. "Hell, this is America," he says vehemently. "Follow our rules or go back where you came from. That's the way I look at it. That's the way my parents looked at it. If you came to this country to better yourself, why complain about it?"

Pride in his country is at the very core of Mr. Tony's character. It's the same loyalty that was instilled in him by his parents after they came to the United States from Sicily in search of a better life. He believes in the American Dream. He has lived it!

GREENBUSH
WOOD PRODUCTS, INC.

Post Office Drawer 340
Abbeville, Alabama 36310
Telephone 205-585-2253

Today is Monday
5 September 1994

Dear James,

I want to tell you how much I enjoyed being with you this past week-end at the Auburn/Ole Miss ball game. It was a close one but hopefully it was due to it being Auburns first SEC game. I feel sure that they will get better as the year progresses.

I know you will do well as an Auburn player because you have the will to the want to and mostly you have the heart and with those attributes and your desire to play and excell I know that with time you will accomplish everything that will be needed of you to make good.

I hesitate to come accross as a preacher, all the same, I think you may profit by a few words of friendly and grandfatherly advice.

Try to be a good listener as you grow older; it is well worth the pains....

Do not get suspicious of people and their motives; and avoid especially prying into the affairs of others...if they ask your help in time of trial, give it in full measure....

Do not try to attract sympathy to yourself in the hope of hearing affectionate murmurs, and above all be a real person with a valuation that does not need artificial boosting.

I would recommend three qualities for you to develop as you grow older: they are Courtesy, Tolerance and Integrity, which together should make you a better well rounded person. These same qualities I have seen in your father. I know your father as a gentleman and a shrewd man of affairs I love and esteem him most highly.

My heart and hand go out to you for all its worth. Grow, be stalwart and hearty; smilefrown not and persevere, and as the years roll round, consider grandmother and me as those who wish you most well.

With all our love,

Dee Dee

Dee Dee

Mr. Tony carries that pride with him everywhere. On a trip to Prague Castle, his youngest son saw that spirit up close. "Dad is one of the proudest men I know," Greg Rane remembers. "Even at 89 years old, he's rough and tough and doesn't take anything off anybody." In Prague, the Rane family and several members of a group from the Ranes' company, Great Southern Wood Preserving, were touring a castle. Several groups of tourists were waiting patiently in line to view a special display upstairs. A tour group from Germany, including two former German Army officers who were stationed in the castle during World War II, broke in line, bolting ahead of everyone.

Mr. Tony had no part of that rude behavior. Politely, he confronted the group leader. "Excuse me, sir, we were in line here first. You need to go behind us," Mr. Tony told him. The man retorted in German, and not politely. Mr. Tony's tone changed. "Let me tell you something," he snapped. "We whipped your butt in '45 and I'm not above doing it again right here!" Discretion being the better part of valor, the German group went to the rear.

Be loyal, be compassionate, be respectful. And if these simple life lessons are difficult to embrace, Mr. Tony will help you learn them, one way or another. "Back during World War II, there were people talking against the U.S.," Mr. Tony remembers. "There was a slogan then: 'Love It Or Leave It.' I still feel that way today. I'm an American who is proud to be an Italian, but I am an American first, last and foremost. But fiercely proud of my Italian heritage. I was in the service for six years and loved it. Nobody likes war. Nobody wants to go to war, but sometimes it is necessary. I believe in America – I always have and always will."

From a rough and tumble childhood in Greenbush to the big city lights of New York to the little Alabama town of Abbeville, Mr. Tony has enhanced the lives of everyone he has touched. He has been a remarkably successful businessman as well as a community and state leader. But most of all, and dearest to his heart, he has been a rock of strength and stability, a cauldron of love and affection, for a family that extends far beyond his wife and two sons.

Mr. Tony has taken his grandchildren and his great-grandchildren under his wing and shared the wisdom of his 89 years by instilling in each of them his values of hard work, honesty, loyalty, and dedication to God and country. He has made his own life a shining example of the possibilities available to each and every one.

From the time he was young, Mr. Tony was fascinated with the world around him, and that same fascination urges him to jump out of bed in the morning as if a surprise is waiting just beyond the front door. "As long as you feel like you can still learn, you are still growing, "Mr. Tony says. "To this day, I still believe you grow as long as you are green. There is something new to learn every day

Mr. Steve Sasso, President of the Italian Workmen's Club, presents Mr. Tony with the first-ever Italian Workmen's Club President's Award.

Frank and Mr. Tony share some Greenbush memories at the President's Award dinner.

in this era of technology. It's amazing what potential there is.

"He was never content with accepting his lot in Madison, but was always in search of the 'pot of gold at the end of the rainbow,' so to speak," says brother Frank. "He was always curious what lay ahead." However, Mr. Tony and his roots are burrowed deep in Greenbush soil.

Mr. Tony has maintained close ties with his childhood friends, many who are members of Madison's Italian Workmen's Club. And from a small, friendly town in a faraway state, Mr. Tony has diligently supported the Club's pet project – the scholarship fund – by generously donating, enabling scores of worthy young men and women to obtain higher education.

The Italian Workmen's Club recently established the President's Award in Mr. Tony's honor. "It's an honor not to be taken lightly," says Frank, "as it will be given only to an individual who leaves a mark of significant importance, one that goes well beyond personal gratification."

This is the second award presented to Mr. Tony from the Club (the first – Columbian of the Year in 1990), and his words are heartfelt: "I am deeply humbled to receive this award, especially as the first-time recipient. Many years have passed since I grew up in the 'Bush, but its influence is as important to me now as it ever was. The things I learned there – the lessons of life and business – have always stayed with me. Take a good look at this punk kid from the 'best part of Madison – Greenbush,' and imagine what has been achieved. Without this community, it could not have been possible. I didn't know it at the time, but our community was the best training ground for success that I could ever have. I was and am blessed by Greenbush. A person should never forget where they came from.

"Of the many gracious awards I've received, these mean more than any.

"You know, I've got two strapping sons who graduated from Auburn University and Harvard University. I asked them to help me with my speech but they wouldn't. That's ok – when they want my spaghetti sauce to impress one of their big clients from Brazil or somewhere…I'll get even."

All roads lead to somewhere, and Mr. Tony has followed many of them. But the road to home is his most traveled and beloved. "My days have been filled with adventures beyond my expectations," remarks Mr. Tony. "Never in the world could I have dreamed of being in this position today. I never thought I'd see my kids graduate from college and live to know all of my beautiful grandchildren. It's been a wonderful, exciting journey."

Mr. Tony has seen life from all sides. He's been wealthy and he's been poor. He's seen joy and heartache, but he's always gone forward with his head held high and his eye on the prize. That's because Mr. Tony knows the value of living each day from the heart, and in the heart of all great men, the chamber reserved for love is the biggest of all.

Mr. Tony: "Life is brighter when hearts are lighter."

The saucepot

is large enough to bathe two babies in and still have room for the family dog. Mr. Tony's tomato sauce is made in huge batches, simmers all day long, and is full of, well, ingredients that remain a family secret. "Basil. Lots of basil. I'll tell you that much," says Mr. Tony. "It doesn't matter whether it's fresh or dry. I prefer dry. Just use a lot of it." No more hints are divulged. The making of the sauce is a family tradition, and the process has been recorded as a part of the Rane family history. "These are the things that money can't buy," says Jimmy. "We emphasize attention on things that are not purchasable because they last."

The Rane family gathers this Sunday for perfectly cooked pasta laden with tomato sauce, Mr. Tony's secret salad dressing, and a little red wine. Decoding the ingredients to Mr. Tony's recipes will require the services of a chemist with an advanced degree in deciphering. He has even been offered money for his salad dressing recipe. His secrets are sought after by food company moguls, but they remain safe with the Rane family.

We all sneak a trip through Mr. Tony and Ms. Libba's kitchen to lift the lid from the pot, to stir the sauce. Conversation stops as the aroma of love wafts through the house. Stomachs begin to rumble. The plates are served as wine glasses are filled. Food and family are blessed, and then, the toast: "La famiglia! La famiglia!"

We are all included now. We are family. We are blessed. Mr. Tony shares his sweet life with all of us.

Acknowledgments

The past has a way of dulling memories that should be kept alive and vibrant for future generations. It is my hope that future generations of my family will always remember the price their ancestors paid to build a better life. Pulling together the details for this project has been a wonderful walk down memory lane for me. I've made every effort to be as accurate as possible and hope the reader will not judge too harshly any forgotten name, date or event.

There are so many people to thank. Joseph and Concetta; Libba, the love of my life; my boys, Jimmy and Greg; all my grandchildren and great-grandchildren; my brother, Frank, and all my family and friends from the 'Bush; friends and associates I served with and worked with and played with; Dale Robertson for his kind words and friendship; the many people who have extended me a "helping hand" over the years. You know who you are and I thank you. It's my hope that I've repaid your generosity by doing the same for others; I also thank Abbeville and all its wonderful people for adopting me so many years ago.

I never knew until now how much work was involved in the making of a book. It has been my privilege and joy to share my life with some wonderfully talented people. Among them are Phillip Marshall to whom a special thanks is owed for undertaking the initial research that was pivotal in getting us started, James Riley for shepherding the project, and my friends at Cottagegate Publishing, Ricky Perkins and Rick Douglas. Thank you both for your care and dedication to the design of this book. And, of course, to Lynn Byrd whose passion for writing knows no boundaries.

And lastly, my gratitude to the Italian Workmen's Club for recently recognizing me with the President's Recognition Award. The lessons that 'I've learned' and have shared with my family are in large part the credit of the Italian community of Greenbush.

Thank you all.

A. J. "Tony" Rane